in_focus

Information
Lives
of the Poor

in_focus

IDRC's *in_focus* Collection tackles current and pressing issues in sustainable international development. Each publication distills IDRC's research experience with an eye to drawing out important lessons, observations, and recommendations. Each also serves as a focal point for an IDRC website that probes more deeply into the issue, and is constructed to serve the differing information needs of IDRC's various readers. A full list of *in_focus* websites may be found at **www.idrc.ca/in_focus**. Each *in_focus* book may be browsed and ordered online at **www.idrc.ca/books**.

IDRC welcomes any feedback on this publication. Please direct your comments to The Publisher at **info@idrc.ca**.

in_focus

Information
Lives
of the Poor

FIGHTING POVERTY WITH TECHNOLOGY

Laurent Elder, Rohan Samarajiva,
Alison Gillwald, and Hernán Galperin

INTERNATIONAL DEVELOPMENT RESEARCH CENTRE
Ottawa • Cairo • Montevideo • Nairobi • New Delhi

Published by the International Development Research Centre
PO Box 8500, Ottawa, ON, Canada K1G 3H9
www.idrc.ca / info@idrc.ca

Library and Archives Canada Cataloguing in Publication

Elder, Laurent, 1971-
Information lives of the poor: fighting poverty with technology /
Laurent Elder, Rohan Samarajiva, Alison Gillwald and Hernán Galperin.

(In focus)
Issued also in French under title: Les pauvres et l'information, combattre
la pauvreté par la technologie; and in Spanish under title: Los pobres en la era
de la información, combatiendo la pobreza con tecnología.
Available also on the Internet.
Includes bibliographical references.
ISBN 978-1-55250-571-7

1. Information technology—Economic aspects—Developing countries.
2. Technological innovations—Economic aspects—Developing countries.
3. Digital divide—Economic aspects—Developing countries.
4. Technology and state—Developing countries.
I. International Development Research Centre (Canada)
II. Title.
III. Title: Fighting poverty with technology.
IV. Series: In focus (International Development Research Centre (Canada))

HC59.72 I55 E43 2013   303.48'33091724   C2013-980084-0
ISBN (ebook) 978-1-55250-574-8

This publication may be read online at **www.idrc.ca/books**, and serves as
the focal point for a thematic website: **www.idrc.ca/in_focus_information.**

MIX
Paper from
responsible sources
FSC
www.fsc.org
FSC® C100205

Contents

Part 3. Current and potential uses of ICTs by the poor ➤ 19

The unique household surveys conducted with IDRC support reveal how and why the developing-country poor are using modern communication tools. The research also highlights regional variations and uncovers evidence linking ICTs and poverty alleviation.

Part 4. Lessons for policymakers ➤ 59

Analysis of the survey results from Africa, Asia, and Latin America provides lessons about how government, civil society, and the private sector can all play a role in ensuring greater social inclusion in the benefits of ICT access.

Part 5. The future ➤ 69

Crowdsourcing and open learning. Censorship and cyber warfare. Technology has both democratic potential and dark sides. This final chapter reflects on the promise and perils of ICTs for the poor in the developing world and recommends some future directions for research.

Glossary of terms and abbreviations ➤ 79

Sources and resources ➤ 81

Executive Summary

The issue

Information and communication have always opened opportunities for the poor to earn income, reduce isolation, and respond resiliently to disasters, conflicts, and emergencies. With mobile phone use exploding across the developing world, even marginalized communities are benefiting from modern communication tools. Some of the world's poorest people now spend substantial portions of their income to make a mobile phone call or go online.

This book explores the impacts of this unprecedented technological change. Drawing on unique household surveys undertaken by research networks active in 38 developing countries, it helps to fill knowledge gaps about how the poor use information and communication technologies (ICTs). How have they benefited from mobile devices, computers, and the Internet? What insights can research provide to promote affordable access to ICTs, so that communities across the developing world can take advantage of the opportunities they offer?

The research

The core of this book synthesizes the findings from groundbreaking research conducted in Africa, Asia, and Latin America with the support of Canada's International Development

Research Centre. Surveys and studies conducted by three regional networks explored the ICT use and spending patterns of the poor and sought to measure the benefits. This volume compiles the evidence across regions and brings together regional perspectives on this important topic.

The researchers found the biggest obstacle to ICT access is cost, and yet cost has not stopped the poor from purchasing phone time. The lowest-earning 75% of mobile phone users in Africa spent large proportions of their household income on communications, as high as 27% for Kenyans. The ability to buy small amounts of prepaid calling time has enabled the very poor in many countries to gain access to mobile phones. In Latin America, however, high taxes on communication services impede some of that access, with a typical broadband plan costing 66% more than in the average developed country. In Asia, meanwhile, a low-cost business model has driven high mobile use.

The poor use phones primarily for social calls, but potential emergencies consistently rank high on surveys as the main reason for buying a phone. For businesses, saving time and money on transportation has emerged as the greatest economic benefit of mobile phone ownership. The increasing number of people accessing the Internet has helped small and home-based businesses, while the mobile phone industry has generated many jobs that serve the sector. Meanwhile, "mobile money" has gained in popularity, suiting the needs of the poor better than conventional banking.

The researchers found links between ICT access and reduced poverty among the very poor. One recent three-year study, for example, followed a large cohort of Peruvians who became Internet users and compared them with non-users in the same period. The household incomes of Internet users were 19% higher, on average, than those who remained non-users. In a study of two villages in Tanzania, residents of one village received five months of mobile phone airtime and Internet access, while the other villagers did not. The first village experienced a reduction in all seven of the poverty criteria used, while changes were seen in only two of the indicators in the second village. The researchers also found that despite the near ubiquity of mobile phones in the developing world, certain groups still have less access, particularly women, the rural poor, and the elderly.

The lessons

The research presented in this book catalyzed policy changes that helped improve access to ICTs by all levels of society. The findings provide useful lessons for policymakers who want to ensure that modern communication tools and information networks benefit all communities, including the most marginalized. Here are some practical steps that can be taken toward achieving that goal:

➤ Open telecommunications markets to competition so that prices come down. Issuing new licences to telecommunications players is the most readily available intervention.

➤ Give regulatory authorities a strong hand in obtaining the information researchers need to better understand the connection between ICTs and poverty alleviation, which in turn will help to inform effective pro-poor communications policies.

➤ Support the ICT sector with government funding to help with infrastructure costs.

➤ Reduce taxes on communication services, which should be seen as vital for society, rather than a luxury.

➤ Nurture the creation of useful content. Promote decentralized innovation by supporting incubators, fostering interactions among entrepreneurs, and encouraging investors.

➤ Offer training in basic computer literacy and the skills needed to fulfill job requirements.

➤ Recognize that solutions must be adapted to local conditions if they are to succeed. There are no one-size-fits-all policy or regulatory responses.

Foreword

How can the poor improve their lot? On a small scale, we have
seen this accomplished through modest gestures. Lending a small
sum that allows someone to buy a few chickens and a cow can
generate enough money to repay the loan and provide a sustainable income. Micro-loans have been an important catalyst in
alleviating poverty.

We have also seen how the explosion in mobile phone use has
helped the poorest sector of the economy. In this book from the
International Development Research Centre, the authors describe
some of the ways mobile phones have improved the lives of the
poor. For example, the leader of a Peruvian peasant-policing group
relates the difficulty of communicating in the hills before mobile
phones. His people had to use whistles and lanterns or light fires
to signal the seriousness of a problem. The case of a 71-year-old
West African man communicating with his wife while travelling
to receive cancer treatment reminds us how vital the mobile phone

can be on a personal level as well. And that the smallest businesses are able to take advantage of new communication technologies is illustrated by the fact that some of the world's poorest people use mobile phones the most.

Doctors reaching their patients more easily or the working poor safely and cheaply transferring their money through mobile phone operators — in these and many other ways, technology can benefit the poor. The poorest of the poor now use phones regularly and thus have become a viable market for telecommunications operators in the developing world. This extra attention gives the poor some clout and much-needed respect. However, according to research reported in this book, they often spend an inordinately high proportion of their income to meet their communication needs.

I'm proud to report that phone ownership among the poorest in my country, Bangladesh, has increased significantly, and we are witnessing the resulting social change. I'm also happy to see the role of the Grameen Village Phone program and its "phone ladies," our front-line workers, acknowledged in this book. Their ability to provide phone time in their villages has been a successful model that is now being replicated in several countries where the phone is still not ubiquitous — in certain African villages, for example.

This book outlines the important role technology plays in poverty alleviation. It also notes that information and communication technology policies are not the solution to everything — to addressing gender inequalities, for example. But the authors do shed considerable light on how technological successes, such as the use of mobile phones, can go a long way toward bridging economic gaps and enabling the poor to improve their lot.

Muhammad Yunus
Nobel Peace Prize Laureate
Founder of the Grameen Bank and Chair of the Yunus Centre

Preface

Why should we care about how the poor access and communicate information? Intuitively, feeling safe and secure, obtaining clean water and food, and preventing sickness and disease appear to be much more important objectives for the poor.

Yet, all of these things are enabled or facilitated by information and communication. Families need to be connected when emergencies, disasters, or conflicts occur. Farmers must know where they can get the best prices for their produce. Health workers need to know, quickly and accurately, where a disease outbreak is occurring.

What's more, the process of exchanging information has gone through a revolution in the past decade. Mobile phones have gone from being a luxury item to one commonly used by most people around the world. Mobiles are now crucial to collecting and communicating information, so much so that economist

Jeffrey Sachs described mobile phones as "the single most transformative technology for development."

Considering the importance of information, communication, and the technologies that enable them, IDRC has supported a vast array of research in this area. From its inception, IDRC focused on information sciences that explored how emerging ICTs enabled researchers around the world to carry out their work in global networks.

The Information and Communication Technologies for Development (ICT4D) program area was a prime example of IDRC's field-building efforts. Through this program, IDRC supported developing-country researchers who realized that if the ICT era passed them and their organizations by — creating the so-called digital divide — it would have a dramatic impact on informed policymaking, research for development, and development itself. Thus, ICT4D's early tactic was to concentrate on research that investigated the regulatory and policy environment, and pursued innovative approaches to the physical infrastructure necessary for providing broad access to the technology.

This approach helped form networks and think tanks in the developing world that specialized in exploring the myriad ways people access and use ICTs. These included three organizations whose research is highlighted in this book:

→ Research ICT Africa (RIA), based in South Africa

→ Learning Initiatives on Reforms for Network Economies Asia (LIRNE*asia*) in Sri Lanka

→ Diálogo Regional sobre la Sociedad de la Información (DIRSI) in Latin America.

These groups undertook groundbreaking research that dispelled myths about the extent to which households in the global South use mobile devices and the Internet, traced the ICT spending patterns of the poor, and measured how they benefited from these technologies. More important, the findings helped catalyze the reform of communications policies to facilitate access by the poor to information networks.

This book is the first compilation of evidence and lessons on this vital topic to bring together regional perspectives in a format accessible to those who need to better understand these issues: government policymakers, donors, and non-governmental organizations that want to ensure that all communities in the developing world have affordable access to the opportunities offered by ICTs.

I would like to thank all the people involved in putting this book together. Philip Fine did the heavy lifting behind the scenes. Kelly Haggart was an able and vigilant task manager who provided crucial input. Finally, there would not have been a book to write without the important work done by the teams led by my co-authors Rohan Samarajiva, Alison Gillwald, and Hernán Galperin. Thank you all.

Laurent Elder
Program Leader, Information and Networks
International Development Research Centre

Part 1

The issues and the development context

Wireless signals, changed lives

Around the planet, bundles of data fly through the air on invisible waves and enter billions of lives. Just a decade ago, few wireless signals were travelling around the developing world. Today, however, information and communication technologies (ICTs) such as mobile phones, computers, and the Internet appear to be everywhere, adapting to a range of lives and livelihoods.

Consider, for example, the Bangladeshi shopkeeper who no longer has to close his store while he goes to buy supplies — now he simply makes a phone call to have them delivered. ICTs have also changed the work of the Peruvian community health nurse, who says mobile phone calls have increased the number of medically assisted births in her rural county and reduced the number of infant deaths to zero. Elsewhere, computers and mobile phones have helped to create informal job markets, organize collective action, or alert neighbours to a cattle rustler. Although many people are still excluded from ownership and many owners can only afford to pay for a minuscule amount of phone time or Internet access, ICTs nevertheless have become entrenched in the lives of people across the developing world.

One device dominates

In the developing world, one information and communication technology dominates all others in the amount of use it receives: the mobile phone. Despite radio's popularity and the tremendous growth in the Internet in much of the developing world, the mobile phone most often acts as the platform from which all other ICTs work. From their phone handsets, a growing number of people in low-income households browse the Internet, send email, text, tweet, keep in touch using Facebook or Mxit, listen to radio, send mobile money, or live chat. Laptops and desktops trail behind the mobile phone as the device from which most people in the developing world control their communications. The first accessible ICT for people in many villages around the world, the mobile phone has reached a great many people in a very short time.

Figure 1. Rate of growth in the use of various technologies

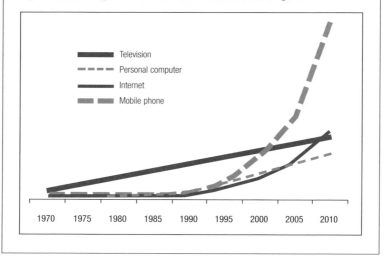

Mobile phone use now extends to those living on a couple of dollars a day. The cost of making a phone call has decreased, thanks to several factors. These include changes in government policies that have increased competition among telecommunications operators and major investments in infrastructure by the private sector. Meanwhile, prepaid cards that allow users to buy small amounts of phone time and the calling-party-pays model, where the recipient of the call is not charged, have allowed more use by the poor.

Evidence shows that widespread use of mobile phones and the Internet could help the poor increase their earning opportunities and eventually find their way out of economic hardship. Social relationships remain a key factor linking widespread ICT access with poverty alleviation. People who keep in touch with others forge important bonds that help them occupy a more secure place in their community. They build stronger networks, as well as the benefits referred to as social capital. They can be reached more easily, and their needs are better known by the people with whom they communicate.

These relationships lay the groundwork for people with few resources to earn money. For example, a day labourer who owns a phone receives a call from a family member with whom he stays in touch. His brother-in-law has just run into a contractor who is looking for a couple of men to pour concrete for a new building. The brother-in-law passes this tip along thanks to the relationship the two have established and the speed with which they can get in touch

Poverty alleviation and ICT access

The International Development Research Centre (IDRC) has funded a number of initiatives that explore poverty alleviation and ICT access. Household surveys and policy analyses in Africa, Asia, and Latin America have examined in depth how ICT access changes the lives of the poor.

Some of this research has focused on whether improvements linked to ICT investment reach those at the bottom of the pyramid (BoP), the term some economists use to describe those in the lowest income bracket.[1] For example, researchers want to understand how ICTs can spur economic growth that benefits the poor. This research, the issues it raises, and the trends it tracks are detailed in Part 3.

Earlier studies provide some evidence that investing in ICTs can improve a nation's economic health:

➤ Using data from 28 developing countries, Sridhar and Sridhar (2007) found that an increase in the number of phones, both fixed-line and mobile, has a positive impact on national economic output.

➤ Waverman et al. (2005) showed that, in a typical developing country, an extra 10 mobile phones per 100 people results in 0.6% growth in per capita GDP. This is double the expected impact in a developed country.

➤ Looking at 113 countries over 20 years, the International Food Policy Research Institute (Torero and Von Braun 2006) found that a 1% increase in telecommunications penetration led to a 0.03% increase in GDP.

---

[1] The bottom of the pyramid, also known as the base of the pyramid, is a concept coined by the late University of Michigan scholar C.K. Prahalad in his book *The Fortune at the Bottom of the Pyramid*. Different studies and surveys, including the ones described in this book, define those at the bottom of the pyramid using different income thresholds, ranging from US$1.25 to US$2.50 a day.

→ A World Bank (2010) study in Kenya calculated that ICTs were responsible for roughly a quarter of Kenya's GDP growth during the first decade of the 21st century.

Mobile phone brings a better price for fish

Fishers in the developing world have traditionally contended with market uncertainty for their perishable stock. Relying on the local market can result in more fish than customers can buy in one town, and insufficient supply for willing buyers in another. The result: income fluctuations for fishing boat operators and workers, and discarded fish where there is a surplus.

In a seminal study, US researcher Robert Jensen (2007) followed a group of 300 fishing units (individual boats as well as operations that brought together several vessels and nets) in the southern Indian state of Kerala, conducting weekly surveys from 1996 to 2001.

Mobile phone service was introduced in the region in 1997, and fishing boat operators quickly began to take advantage of the service to communicate with buyers on shore. The money spent on the phones proved to be well worth the investment. Jensen reported a 9% increase in weekly profits for the fishing units and an end to uneven prices after the introduction of mobile phones.

Jensen's work has been cited often to show a clear link between mobile phone use and improved livelihoods in the developing world. Fishers on the boats were able to communicate with buyers in neighbouring towns and decide where to dock based on the expected price for their catch. As a result, 30–40% of them delivered to buyers outside the "catchment zone" near their towns. The usual dumping of 5–8% of the catch was completely eliminated, resulting in zero waste.

The study, which also noted a small saving for consumers, ruled out other explanations for the changes and concluded that the introduction of the mobile phone had led to the improvements in the market. As Jensen suggested, this experience could be replicated in other situations where using mobile phones could help regulate the prices of both perishable and non-perishable goods.

On the web **THE ISSUE**

Other researchers argue that investment in ICTs cannot thrive in a vacuum, but must be accompanied by other investments or initiatives. For example, Duncombe (2006) contends that ICT applications may reduce poverty, but only if accompanied by a broad range of social and political changes. He found that they would be more effective if used as a means to build programs and resources that benefit the poor. An increasing number of researchers agree that investment in ICTs brings some benefit to the poor, particularly if it is part of larger and more comprehensive economic and social investments aimed at alleviating poverty.

Taking research questions into the home

How does investment in ICTs lead to economic gains for developing countries? This question has generated much debate in academic circles as the studies by Waverman et al. (2005) and Duncombe (2006) indicate. However, further questions need to be answered to inform these debates and assess whether ICT use and ownership improves conditions for the poor. This is where qualitative studies — household or user-focused studies, or smaller community-level ones such as Jensen's — become invaluable. They help to explain more clearly how ICTs may play a role in reducing poverty.

Even if we accept that greater access to ICTs leads to economic gains, ICT ownership remains unaffordable for millions of people and the cost of regularly using a phone can be onerous. Yet, many people in developing countries do covet mobile phones and spend substantial portions of their income to use them. What insights, then, can research provide to help ensure greater access to ICTs?

With this in mind, IDRC-supported researchers have taken survey questions into the homes and workplaces of ICT users to determine the economic and social impacts of these technologies. Tracking changes at the macro level is important. Equally, if not more important is hearing individuals' stories by asking a host of questions about their experiences. For example:

→ How has your life been changed by having access to a mobile phone or the Internet?

→ Have ICTs helped you feel less isolated?

→ How has the mobile phone improved your business?

→ What strategies do you use to keep communication costs down?

→ Do you feel overly tethered to your electronic device?

As the field of ICT for development expands and new research emerges, further questions arise:

→ What conditions are needed to increase ownership or provide greater access for those who find phone use too expensive?

→ Although a positive correlation between a country's GDP and investment in ICTs and their infrastructure has been demonstrated, how will the prosperity spread to the poor?

→ How, and how much, should governments and donors invest in ICT infrastructure?

→ How can the benefits of the mobile phone revolution become inclusive?

→ Do those investing in e-health, e-agriculture, and e-education understand how beneficiaries of these programs are using these ICTs?

→ How do communities in different regions of the world access and use ICTs?

→ What are good practices for governments, donors, and the private sector?

→ What are the opportunities and threats for the developing world with respect to this new access to ICTs?

Part 2

The approach

Critical areas for research

Telecommunications networks and services are vital for a nation's information needs and can lead to a robust information economy. Much of the necessary transformation to an information economy begins with telecommunications reform. This generally consists of the following steps (although there is some debate about their sequence): freeing up the market for the entry of new ICTs, creating an independent regulator, and privatizing the state-owned operator.

Although developing-country governments may be keen to bridge the digital divide, to be socially inclusive, and to build knowledge societies, achieving these goals means making changes.

To establish a competitive environment, policies and regulations must be revamped in the face of three principal challenges:

➤ The pace of technological change is so rapid that many have difficulty understanding its implications.

➤ The evidence to inform effective decisions is often lacking.

➤ Even when evidence supports change, resistance may persist.

Research networks based in the global South

In this section, we introduce a global network of researchers helping to fill important information gaps in the developing world. IDRC has supported the creation of regional research networks in Africa, Asia, and Latin America and the Caribbean that are building a critical mass of evidence on ICTs for development.

Research ICT Africa (RIA), Learning Initiatives on Reforms for Network Economies Asia (LIRNE*asia*), and Diálogo Regional sobre la Sociedad de la Información (DIRSI) focus on telecommunications reform and the spread of ICT infrastructure in the developing world (Figure 2). These networks work to better understand the factors that lead to improved ICT access and use by the poor, and their links to poverty alleviation. They have used innovative survey methodologies to uncover new information and help to inform pro-poor policies. These surveys and their findings are discussed in detail in Part 3.

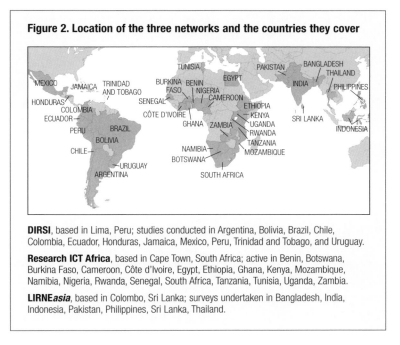

Figure 2. Location of the three networks and the countries they cover

DIRSI, based in Lima, Peru; studies conducted in Argentina, Bolivia, Brazil, Chile, Colombia, Ecuador, Honduras, Jamaica, Mexico, Peru, Trinidad and Tobago, and Uruguay.

Research ICT Africa, based in Cape Town, South Africa; active in Benin, Botswana, Burkina Faso, Cameroon, Côte d'Ivoire, Egypt, Ethiopia, Ghana, Kenya, Mozambique, Namibia, Nigeria, Rwanda, Senegal, South Africa, Tanzania, Tunisia, Uganda, Zambia.

LIRNE*asia*, based in Colombo, Sri Lanka; surveys undertaken in Bangladesh, India, Indonesia, Pakistan, Philippines, Sri Lanka, Thailand.

Research ICT Africa, a South Africa-based network of researchers in 19 African countries, conducts research on ICT policy and regulation. It advocates improved access to ICTs and conducts research on policies and regulations that responds to national, regional, and continental needs. The RIA network has built up a repository of up-to-date ICT data and analysis that helps inform innovative and appropriate policies. Its work has created a cadre of African policy experts who engage with decision-makers to build enabling policy and regulatory environments.

LIRNE*asia*, a think tank based in Sri Lanka, works actively across the Asia-Pacific region studying ICT policy and regulation. It seeks to improve lives in the region by increasing the use of ICTs and related infrastructure. Its goal is to reform laws, policies, and regulations through research, training, and advocacy, while build-ing a team of ICT policy and regulatory professionals in the region. LIRNE*asia* seeks to change the aspects of ICT governance and regulation that inhibit and obstruct access to ICTs, replacing them with policies that improve lives and increase access.

DIRSI is a Latin American network that brings together professionals and institutions specializing in ICT policy and research. It conducts research, publishes and distributes papers and reports, and facilitates dialogue on ICT policy, regulation, and governance in the region. Through this work, DIRSI supports the development of policies aimed at enabling Latin America's marginalized communities to participate effectively in the new information economy.

The need for household-level information

RIA, LIRNE*asia*, and DIRSI soon realized that to catalyze reforms that would truly benefit the poor and increase their access to ICTs, they needed accurate and timely data on how ICTs were being used. They also needed to understand the factors contributing to the marginalization of the poor. With accurate data, they could convince policymakers to undertake pro-poor reforms and argue against measures that disadvantage the poor.

Statistics agencies in developing countries do not generally collect adequate data on ICT use and access in their household surveys or national census. Although a few donor agencies have conducted surveys on ICT use, the small sample sizes have made these difficult to generalize to the country level. The only global institution responsible for collecting ICT data is the International Telecommunication Union (ITU), but its findings are limited to supply-side data. These statistics, which originate from telecommunications operators, are often incomplete and, in some cases, flawed. Supply-side indicators do not reveal how much households spend on ICTs, what they use them for, whether ICTs help improve their livelihoods, or how various members of a household use ICTs.

The World Summit on the Information Society's Measuring the Information Society initiative, led by the ITU and the United Nations Conference on Trade and Development, has developed international indicators and model surveys. It has also helped to train national statistics officers. However, few developing countries have made use of these resources.

Governments frequently react to increased mobile penetration by raising taxes on equipment and communications. When this happens, groups need to demonstrate the benefits of mobiles for the poor, such as how they help improve livelihoods or contribute to empowerment and resilience. They also need to argue against taxes on such services that disproportionately affect the poor.

Data on ICT use are also essential for country comparisons. In some parts of the world, one of the best ways to spur policy reform is to shame governments into action by comparing them to countries with better records. Being identified as a country with one of the worst rates of access or highest ICT costs can help to propel policy change. On the other hand, some argue that shaming can backfire by putting politicians on the defensive, causing them to accuse researchers of trying to Westernize the country or force it into a free-market straitjacket.

Collecting household data

Africa

RIA undertook a series of demand-side surveys of ICT access and use in an effort to better understand how ICT services are being used in Africa. In 2004, surveys were carried out in 10 countries, involving 12,000 households. In 2007–2008, 23,000 households in 17 countries were canvassed. The data collected included gender, age, and education, as well as information on household income and assets. The later survey was fleshed out with focus group studies in five countries that specifically addressed gender issues.

In 2011–2012, RIA undertook a third survey of about 14,000 households in 11 African countries. The network also piggybacked on an informal-sector and micro-business survey, which included the types of enterprises found in residential areas.

The RIA questionnaires were divided into three sections. The first collected information about all household members. The second collected other household-related information. These sections were answered by the head of the household or someone who manages the household. The third part, the individual section, was answered by a randomly selected household member, 16 years of age or older. It collected information on all household members and visitors.

The surveys were conducted in person, to guarantee maximum response rates. Protecting data is a key challenge, as hardware might fail or get stolen and databases may be corrupted. In some countries, the household survey was conducted in cooperation with the national statistics office (NSO). In Tanzania, for example, the NSO conducted the survey for RIA. In other countries, including Ghana, Kenya, Mozambique, and Zambia, NSO staff assisted with the survey. However, overall the NSO played a limited role and, in some jurisdictions, displayed resistance by choosing not to collaborate in implementing the surveys. For the 2011–2012 survey, fieldwork and data collection were outsourced to market research companies across the continent, although this required extensive training in research protocols. RIA carried out all the sampling and weighting of the data.

To further investigate the links between ICT access and poverty alleviation, IDRC also supported Poverty and ICTs in Urban and Rural Eastern Africa (PICTURE Africa). Using qualitative and quantitative data gathered at the household level over time, this initiative explored how and whether access to ICTs helps to reduce poverty in urban and rural households in four East African countries.

Previous data analyses had looked at fairly simple relationships between ICT ownership, penetration, or investment and broad economic indicators such as GDP growth. However, variations in individuals' well-being are not necessarily linked to changes in GDP at the national level. Thus, it is important to go beyond national-level growth and look at the impact of ICTs on poverty reduction at the micro level.

With this in mind, PICTURE Africa used data collected from households in Kenya, Rwanda, Tanzania, and Uganda in 2007 and 2010. Researchers also looked at two comparable communities over time: one with significant ICT access and one without. PICTURE Africa was able to draw conclusions about inequalities in ICT access in East Africa, the impediments to more equitable access, and, most notably, the extent to which ICTs were a determining factor in the resilience of poor communities.

Asia

LIRNE*asia*'s Teleuse@BOP surveys investigate the use of ICTs in South Asia, the region with the largest concentration of poor people in the world. Four surveys between 2005 and 2011 tracked individuals and households whose earnings put them at the bottom of the pyramid in South and Southeast Asia. In South Asia, the three most populous countries were included — India, Pakistan, and Bangladesh — as well as Sri Lanka. When the surveys were first launched in 2005, Nepal proved to be a difficult place to conduct fieldwork because of civil conflict, and it was omitted. Parts of Pakistan and Sri Lanka also had to be excluded at certain times for the same reason. In Southeast Asia, the Philippines was included in 2006 and 2008, Indonesia in 2011, and Thailand in all three years.

These Teleuse@BOP surveys have focused on people who made or received a call within the previous three months. Participants were not limited to subscribers or owner-users, but also included those who were, or were not, planning to become owners. Information has been collected (in six languages) from about 10,000 respondents.

Qualitative studies have also been conducted. They offer a snapshot of phone habits, allowing researchers to better understand the effects of the rapid spread of mobile phones, especially in countries where teleuse is still not universal.

Latin America

In Latin America, a different approach was taken. With support from IDRC, the United Nations Economic Commission for Latin America and the Caribbean (ECLAC) compiled household data on ICT use and access. This data was drawn from national household surveys and national innovation surveys conducted by government statistics offices. The project, entitled Observatory for the Information Society in Latin America and the Caribbean, helped shed light on the ICT revolution by enabling researchers to tap into a rich microdata set. DIRSI researchers have used this data extensively, partnering with ECLAC to produce two books that document the progress of the digital revolution on the continent (Jordán et al. 2011, 2013).

However, these surveys included only a limited number of questions about ICT use. To examine the patterns of such use by the poor, DIRSI also conducted its own surveys. As part of a project called Mobile Opportunities, it interviewed more than 7,000 people from poor neighbourhoods about their use of and expenditures related to ICTs, with a particular focus on mobile telephony. The interviews were conducted in Argentina, Brazil, Colombia, Jamaica, Mexico, Peru, and Trinidad and Tobago.

This fieldwork allowed DIRSI researchers to test hypotheses suggested by an earlier project, Digital Poverty. The key idea was that inequalities related to access and use remained, despite the data showing almost universal adoption of mobile telephony across the continent. DIRSI's survey also showed that mobile phone costs in Latin America were among the highest in the world. It recommended policies to make access more affordable by those at the bottom of the income pyramid.

Mobile Opportunities was followed by a second project, Mobile Opportunities 2.0, which examined specific development opportunities associated with the widespread adoption of mobile telephony. Among the most promising areas identified were mobile banking and the delivery of public services. The findings also revealed a need to reform universal service policies in light of the increased coverage of mobile telephony networks and the shifting patterns of demand in favour of more advanced services such as Internet access.

Currently, DIRSI is engaged in a six-country study of the development impact of broadband focusing on three key areas: employment, poverty reduction, and educational outcomes. The positive impact of broadband on employment and income is quite apparent. However, early evidence shows that gains from broadband adoption in schools are less clear and depend on a number of other changes in the context and the learning experience of students.

THE RESEARCH
On the web

Part 3

Current and potential uses of ICTs by the poor

How the poor use ICTs

Mobile phones everywhere you look

Chickens run around an African village, their clucking pierced by a less traditional rural sound: the ring tone of a mobile phone. In another village, women gather to talk while washing laundry at the river. Their conversation loses a participant as one woman pulls out her phone to take a call. All over the developing world, the mobile phone has found a place alongside the traditional features of rural life.

The mobile phone now plays a vital role in the lives of people at all income levels, and this fact is reflected in statistics showing widespread use. According to the International Telecommunication Union, in 2012 there were 91 mobile subscriptions for every 100 people on earth.

In many of the poorest parts of the world, almost everyone appears to have found some way to access ICTs. A 2011 study by LIRNE*asia* found that 99% of poor Bangladeshis had used a phone in the previous three months (Samarajiva 2011, Teleuse@BOP4). The corresponding figure for Pakistan was 96% and for India, 89%. Although these high rates include both mobile and fixed-line phones, the proliferation of the mobile has increased overall access. This is the case even in Latin America, where costs are much higher than in most other parts of the developing world. "In just a few years, mobile telephony penetration has reached levels far higher than those attained by fixed telephony over several decades," write Bonina and Illa (2008) in a DIRSI paper.

The explosion of mobile phone use has provided wide access to many who never before had the opportunity to use a telephone. For many years, mobiles were thought of as technology for the rich, but they have been adapted to the needs of the poor. Whether it's a community coping with civil war or a mother at work keeping in touch with her children, people everywhere want and need access to reliable communications.

Mobile phones allow the poor to stay in contact with far-flung relatives they depend on for remittances. They can reach people in the next district who typically help out in a crisis or need help themselves. They can call a friend simply to chat. Despite the poor living conditions in one overcrowded house in Namibia's Omifitu village, every adult owns a phone. One Namibian man counted 153 mobile phones among the 154 employees in his office, and he soon owned the 154th.

Not the same information societies

Information societies in the developed world were formed through the rapid spread of computers and the Internet. People in Canada, Norway, and Japan, for example, were first introduced to digital technologies through a desktop computer and an online account. Mobile phones have only recently overtaken computers as the device of choice in those countries. Not so in the developing world, where computers and an Internet connection in the home remain a luxury most people cannot afford. Instead, most Africans and Asians today experience their first contact with the Internet through their mobile phones.

Internet going mobile where it can

Perhaps one of the starkest differences between the RIA surveys conducted in 2007–2008 and in 2011–2012 is the growing Internet access made possible by mobile phones. The 2007–2008 access and use survey showed an alarmingly low rate of Internet access in Africa, along with a large-scale absence of computers and smartphones. That was further compounded by the high cost of connectivity.

Since then, Internet access has grown significantly — to 15.5% across the 11 African countries surveyed in 2011–2012. The mobile phone is now the key entry point for Internet use. This is likely because mobile Internet requires fewer ICT skills and financial resources than desktop or laptop computers and does not rely on having electricity at home. Social networking applications have also boosted the popularity of connecting to the Internet from a mobile phone.

However, unevenness in Internet uptake remains, both across and within countries. Although mobile Internet use has increased in most African countries, going online remains a very infrequent activity for people in Ethiopia, Tanzania, and Rwanda (Figure 3).

On the web

THE RESEARCH

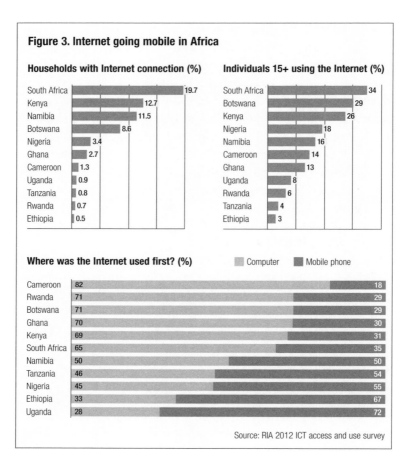

Figure 3. Internet going mobile in Africa

Households with Internet connection (%)

South Africa	19.7
Kenya	12.7
Namibia	11.5
Botswana	8.6
Nigeria	3.4
Ghana	2.7
Cameroon	1.3
Uganda	0.9
Tanzania	0.8
Rwanda	0.7
Ethiopia	0.5

Individuals 15+ using the Internet (%)

South Africa	34
Botswana	29
Kenya	26
Nigeria	18
Namibia	16
Cameroon	14
Ghana	13
Uganda	8
Rwanda	6
Tanzania	4
Ethiopia	3

Where was the Internet used first? (%)　　■ Computer　■ Mobile phone

	Computer	Mobile phone
Cameroon	82	18
Rwanda	71	29
Botswana	71	29
Ghana	70	30
Kenya	69	31
South Africa	65	35
Namibia	50	50
Tanzania	46	54
Nigeria	45	55
Ethiopia	33	67
Uganda	28	72

Source: RIA 2012 ICT access and use survey

The story is similar among the poor in Asia. In Thailand, 78% of the poor surveyed in a 2011–2012 LIRNE*asia* study had never used the Internet, while the figure for Pakistan was 98%. An alarming number had never even heard of the Internet in India (24%) and Bangladesh (17%).

Rates of computer use are also still relatively low across developing countries. Findings from the 2011–2012 RIA survey of 11 African countries show that computer use is above 10% in only four of the countries. Computer use approaches 30% only in South Africa.

In Kenya it is slightly above 21%, in Cameroon 15%, and in Namibia 13% (Calandro et al. 2012). Among the poor in Asia, 21% of Thais and 17% of Sri Lankans had used a computer in the previous year, but only 4% of Pakistanis and 2% of Indians. In India, 16% of the poor had never heard of a computer (LIRNE*Asia*, 2011–2012).

As governments, donors, and non-governmental organizations (NGOs) increasingly invest in technology to help improve conditions in areas such as agriculture, health, education, and gender empowerment, they need to understand how the communities they are trying to help access and use the technology. Without that understanding, their programs are vulnerable to failure.

Women not coming to the phone
Women generally have less access than men to ICTs, and this gap increases as technologies and services become more sophisticated and expensive, according to a gender-specific overview of the 2011–2012 RIA survey (Deen-Swarray et al. 2013). Being female significantly reduces the probability of Internet use, especially in Ethiopia, Ghana, and Nigeria. Women, in general, are less likely to use a computer, although being a married woman in South Africa, Namibia, Kenya, or Nigeria increases the likelihood of computer use. Income is a significant factor contributing to computer use across all countries except Ghana, and education is positively related to computer use in all countries.

Being female and living in a rural setting reduces the chances of gaining access to ICTs by about 50%, according to the four-country studies conducted in 2007 and 2010 by PICTURE Africa (May et al. 2011). In RIA's 17-country study in Africa undertaken in 2007–2008, only half the participants (both men and women) from low-income groups and none of the participants from rural groups had a mobile phone (Gillwald et al. 2010). One woman in Ethiopia, a country where no telecommunications reform has taken place and services are run as a monopoly, put it succinctly when she told RIA: "I want to have a mobile phone but I can't afford it."

What evidence do policymakers need to change this situation? Even group-specific statistics that show men have greater access to ICTs than women can be unhelpful in terms of identifying what needs to be done. This led RIA to conclude that, to a large extent, gender inequities in access and usage cannot be addressed through ICT policies *per se*, but require policy interventions in other areas. However, RIA notes that it is difficult to "legislate away" many of the barriers for women that relate to cultural norms and practices.

RIA's 2011–2012 survey confirms that, with few exceptions, women in the 11 African countries surveyed generally have less access to ICTs than men (Figure 4). Not surprisingly, higher levels of education and income are related to greater access and use of technology, and the proportion of women is greater in the groups with lower levels of education and income. Where education and income are more equal among men and women, access to ICTs is generally higher among women and use is more equitable.

In countries where women are socially constrained, the digital divide is greater, whereas better earning opportunities for women are usually associated with better ICT access. One example of the former situation is Pakistan, where women face restrictions in moving around unchaperoned. Their time is largely dedicated to household chores and child rearing, and men make most of the household spending decisions. These factors contribute to the much lower use of mobile and public phones by Pakistani women. Their time spent on mobile phones often depends on the goodwill of the people who own the devices.

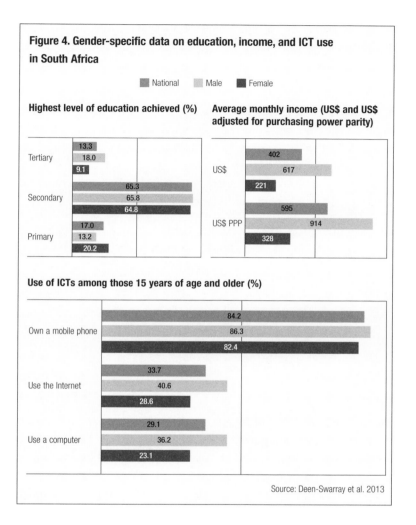

Figure 4. Gender-specific data on education, income, and ICT use in South Africa

■ National   ▨ Male   ■ Female

Highest level of education achieved (%)

	National	Male	Female
Tertiary	13.3	18.0	9.1
Secondary	65.3	65.8	64.8
Primary	17.0	13.2	20.2

Average monthly income (US$ and US$ adjusted for purchasing power parity)

	National	Male	Female
US$	402	617	221
US$ PPP	595	914	328

Use of ICTs among those 15 years of age and older (%)

	National	Male	Female
Own a mobile phone	84.2	86.3	82.4
Use the Internet	33.7	40.6	28.6
Use a computer	29.1	36.2	23.1

Source: Deen-Swarray et al. 2013

In "Who's got the phone? Gender and the use of the telephone at the bottom of the pyramid," Zainudeen et al. (2010) draw on 2006 figures that show a three-to-one ratio of male-to-female phone ownership in Pakistan, with almost four times as many women as men relying on the use of other people's phones. "The core cause of the problem appears to lie outside the realm of telecom, in the subordination of women in economic decision-making within families," the authors write. They suggest that the gender divide could be narrowed somewhat if the cost of handsets was reduced, allowing families to afford a second mobile phone for the woman's use.

LIRNEasia's 2011 Teleuse@BOP survey found that things had improved at the bottom of the pyramid in Pakistan, but not by much. While 86% of the men in the survey made calls from their own phones, only 50% of the women did. Another 25% relied on relatives, friends, and neighbours for making calls, and almost no women made calls from public phones.

Gender differences in ownership, as well as dependence on others for phone use, appear to be less striking in India, and even less so in Sri Lanka. In Thailand, more women own phones than men.

Men spend more money than women on mobile phone use. However, women spend a higher proportion of their income on phone services. Both practices likely stem from the fact that women generally earn less than men.

Sources: LIRNEasia, RIA

Meanwhile, in 14 out of 17 African countries, more men than women own mobile phones, according to the 2007–2008 survey conducted by RIA (Gillwald et al. 2010). The exceptions among the African countries surveyed were South Africa, Mozambique, and Cameroon, where women phone owners outnumber men. In Latin America, a study of Peruvian households by DIRSI (Agüero 2008) found that a household headed by a woman is more likely to spend money on telecommunications than one headed by a man.

A common perception is that women spend most of their time on the phone maintaining relationships, while men use telephones for more functional purposes, such as conducting business. However, LIRNEasia found that, at least in some countries, both genders use telephones for much the same reasons. "Both men and women engaged in relationship maintenance through the phone at more or less the same level in the Indian and Sri Lankan BoP," write Zainudeen et al. (2010). However, they did find that women in Pakistan and the Philippines spend more phone time than men on relationship maintenance.

For women, security remains the main factor in their decision to buy a phone. DIRSI (Galperin and Mariscal 2007) found that women, more than men, say they use mobile phones for emergency situations. But DIRSI's research shows that the main reason both women and men adopt mobile devices is to cope with uncertainty. This is a broader concept than emergencies alone and encompasses the daily challenges the poor face in the developing world, including transportation and informal transactions such as barter and trade.

The gender differences appear more acute when it comes to Internet use. Vergara et al. (2011) found that women are less likely than men to use the Internet, even when access is provided. It also found that women were more likely to use the Internet for activities related to education and training, but less likely to use it for entertainment, banking, and shopping.

Youth embracing ICTs, seniors showing reluctance
Young people appear to be leading the mobile phone revolution. Youth between 18 and 25 years of age are the fastest-growing segment among those at the bottom of the pyramid to adopt mobile devices, according to LIRNE*asia*'s comprehensive five-country study (Teleuse@BOP3 2009). In this sample, the average age for mobile ownership was 22 for men and 24 for women, and most of these young people were the first in their family to buy a phone. Youth also play a big role in many of the decisions surrounding the phone, from which subscriber identity module (SIM) card the family should buy to managing their parents' contacts. The LIRNE*asia* study also found that the older the most senior person in the household using a mobile phone, the younger the age of the child who assists them in using that phone.

In another survey, this one commissioned by RIA, Patience Smith (2011) interviewed dozens of Namibians of all ages about how they use technology. Among youth, she observed, those who see the Internet as a safe place to socialize electronically send friends credit so that they can text with them. Others use late-night discounts for Internet access, then find themselves nodding off in class the next day. Many visit the local university for the wireless access, to recharge their phones, or watch TV. Smith also found that some African youth appear to be obsessed with Facebook. One young man admitted spending 80% of his time on social networks. "I love it," he said. And if he could not use it anymore? "My world would end."

In Asia, similar stories were documented in Teleuse@BOP3 (2009). Like the young people Smith met, who put any extra money they earn toward "tech," many of the youth in the LIRNE*asia* study were saving for one purchase: a mobile phone. Half the young owners surveyed had saved up to buy their phone, while parents helped the other half finance their purchase. Phones can sometimes help circumvent taboos, particularly in Bangladesh and Sri Lanka. In those countries, some young people buy a separate SIM card for the sole purpose of carrying on conversations with a boyfriend or girlfriend their parents might not like.

The intense interest young people take in their phones worries some older people who think they are missing out on childhood fun. One of Smith's interviewees, a farmer named Tobie, bemoaned the behaviour of some teens who stayed indoors all day during a recent visit to his farm. Glued to their mobiles, they were not taking in all the things he says he loved as a child: the fresh air, swimming, and animals.

Despite his reservations about technology, Tobie believes his rural area should be better wired or more young people will leave. "They don't want to struggle under candlelight anymore. They want to be in the cities," he said. Tobie himself has learned to

Skype with his adult children, speaking to them from a friend's house in town. Could investing in rural ICT infrastructure, therefore, be one way to help stem the rural exodus?

Those in Tobie's age, geographic, and income bracket seem to be adapting less readily to another form of communication: short message service (SMS), otherwise known as texting. In a study of SMS use among low-income mobile users in Asia, Kang and Maity (2012) found texters to be primarily young, single city dwellers with relatively high income and more education. "SMS has not reached the majority of the older, poorer, rural people with little or no education," the authors write. They report that those who shy away from SMS tend to do so because they find it technically difficult, not because of its cost or the literacy skills required.

The LIRNE*asia* studies, which covered seven countries in four time periods, looked at the reasons some people did not take to SMS. These were the top three:

➤ They don't understand what it means to text.

➤ They find the technology confusing.

➤ The typing is too difficult.

A DIRSI study conducted among low-income communities in Mexico on perceptions of the benefits of the Internet found that it is seen as a tool for social mobility and that young people are the ones who can best achieve this. For older adults, the Internet represents an alien world and they do not feel they have the skills to benefit from it. However, once young students were taught to help their parents use the Internet, a new world of information opened for the adults. As one of the interviewees, a 43-year-old woman in San Miguel de Allende, put it: "I thought this was only for those who are young ... but then I was taught and I realized I can learn. Then I went to tell my neighbour: 'Look, now I know!'" This testimony highlights the central role of young people as intermediaries in facilitating and guiding the adults' search for information. Moreover, the role of family members as intermediaries proved to be critical as they share common challenges and thus have incentives to search for information that benefits the family (Mariscal and Martínez 2013).

These findings provide important information for governments, NGOs, and donors supporting projects in the field of ICT for development. ICT initiatives intended to improve development outcomes in learning and health programs must be designed in ways that do not further marginalize seniors, women, and rural dwellers.

The poor become an important market

The biggest challenge preventing the poor from accessing ICTs is cost, but cost has not stopped them from purchasing phone time. Even those estimated to be living on a couple of dollars a day have become an important and growing market. The percentage of wages the poorest members of society are prepared to spend on communications was thought to be in the 2–3% range. Many observers now realize how significantly they underestimated the desire for instant communication.

RIA, for example, showed that the lowest-earning 75% of mobile phone users in Africa spent large proportions of their household income on communications, with averages as high as 27% for Kenyans and as low as 11% for South Africans. Expenditures appear to be high in conflict-affected areas as well. A pilot study in Jaffna, Sri Lanka, where much of the conflict between government and Tamil rebels has taken place, found communications costs of 12–15% of household income — higher than in the rest of South Asia (Samarajiva et al. 2008).

In many African countries, the ability to buy small amounts of prepaid calling time has enabled the very poor to gain access to mobiles. However, the cost per second of use is high compared with the rate longer-term subscribers pay. Thus, prepaid users spend more on an individual call or text than people who have the means to pay for a monthly subscription. This discrepancy is changing in many markets where termination charges have been reduced. New sellers have been able to undercut prices charged by the incumbents and gain market share.

In Latin America, although micro-payments have lowered the barrier to access, high taxes on phone services and high mobile interconnection fees put phone use out of reach of those at the bottom of the pyramid. In Africa, meanwhile, low-income house-holds spend a higher proportion of earnings on telecommunica-tions than those with high incomes. However, these African and Latin American trends are not seen in Asia, where a low-cost business model has driven high mobile use.

The high percentage of income spent on telecommunication must be viewed in context. An important hidden factor fuelling spending is remittances received from overseas, which are often not reported as income. Thus, a researcher calculating the pro-portion of income spent on telecommunications may find part of the equation to be unreliable.

In addition, data on use may not be accurate. "Unlike in developed countries where usage is easily obtainable from monthly bills for post-paid connections, the vast majority in developing countries (in the case of the current study this is between 78% and 99%) has no billing records. Many use public phones, phones at work, or other people's phones, which equally does not generate records" (Gillwald and Stork 2008).

How much a poor person would sacrifice for the ability to make a pressing phone call is illustrated by survey responses reported in Samarajiva and Zainudeen (2008). Faced with a dire need for money and calling a relative overseas the only way of obtaining it, some survey participants said they would be willing to spend as much as 6% of their monthly income on one three-minute call.

THE RESEARCH
On the web

In "Can the poor afford mobile telephony? Evidence from Latin America," Barrantes and Galperin (2008) say that, prepaid options aside, the poor are simply spending too much of their income on communication. "Even in countries where mobile services appeared to be more affordable, the cost of a prepaid low-volume basket exceeds 10% of the poverty line, and thus is well beyond the reach of the average poor."

Money spent on communication means less money for essential items. In Uganda, for example, researchers found that ICT use often diverts money from household food budgets (Diga 2013), while the average Chilean spends more on telecommunications than on water (Smith et al. 2011).

Poor people in Latin America tend to bear the highest communication costs. Based on 2009 figures, the average cost of phone service in Latin America is almost twice the average for OECD countries and three times the average for the South Asian market. Costa Rica is the only country in Latin America where phone costs are affordable for low-income earners. The high cost of going online creates another set of challenges for the poor in Latin America.

Latin America pays high price for going online

After years of increasing at rates close to 50%, Internet subscription fees have begun to drop in Latin America, although they are still very high compared with the rest of the world (Figure 5). According to a DIRSI survey, the typical broadband plan in Latin America costs 66% more than in the developed countries of the Organisation for Economic Co-operation and Development (Galperin 2012). The increasing use of bundling options, which provide discounts for grouping several household telecommunications services, offers some hopeful signs that access will increase and prices will continue to drop.

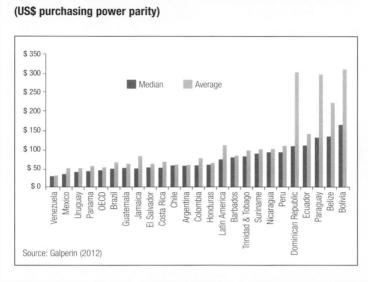

Figure 5. Monthly cost of fixed broadband plans in Latin America, 2012 (US$ purchasing power parity)

■ Median   ▨ Average

Source: Galperin (2012)

Ring me twice: Strategies for saving money

Communication by phone remains financially difficult for many people, which has led to users finding ways to make their purchased phone time stretch further. One way to do that has been through "beeping." A person makes a call on a mobile phone, but hangs up before the recipient answers, leaving the displayed missed call to act as a message between the two parties. Some users have even worked out codes, as a Bangladesh study discovered (Chakraborty 2004). Callers who disconnected after one ring were understood to be saying, "I'm home. Where are you?" Two rings meant, "I'm at your house. Where are you?" Also in Bangladesh, Teleuse@BOP3 researchers discovered that one missed call between friends or spouses meant "I'm thinking of you."

Beeping appears to be used between friends more often than between professional colleagues or elders, although LIRNE*asia* did report a relevant work-related situation in Sri Lanka. When a man named Dharmaratna receives a beep from a carpentry shop that employs him on an occasional basis, he is expected to call the shop owner, and thus pay for the call, if he is interested in work (Teleuse@BOP3 2009).

A strategy often used with friends or relatives who are in a better financial position is to send a text message saying "Please call," putting the onus on the recipient to pay for the call. Street vendors have developed a variation on this. When they want to purchase more phone time, they send a simple text message: "I want to buy now." A vendor then appears with prepaid vouchers, with the user spending very little to order the time. According to the 2007 DIRSI survey, people in Latin America and the Caribbean have found similar ways to use their phones for little or no money. Many of them also beep, signalling that the recipient should call using a public phone.

In many countries, the public pay phone remains the most cost-effective form of telephony, and many mobile phone owners take advantage of that. A common strategy is to send a "want to talk" message using a mobile, but then use a pay phone for the bulk of the conversation. In Tanzania, 96% of those surveyed who owned a mobile phone or SIM card had also used a pay phone in the previous three months, while in Zambia 93% used both devices (Gillwald and Stork 2008). Nevertheless, pay phone use is dwindling across Africa. In RIA's 2011-2012 survey of 11 countries, only about 16% of respondents had used a public phone in the previous three months.

Other cost-saving strategies include capping telephone use at a certain level, restricting calls to a specific group of people, or keeping calls short. Some use the phone for emergency calls only, keeping on reserve as little as 10 cents (US$) in phone time.

Many users at the bottom of the pyramid place few outgoing calls. In the Latin America and Caribbean study involving more than 7,000 people with low incomes (Galperin and Mariscal 2007), researchers found that in most of the seven countries surveyed, more than one-third of respondents had not made a single outgoing call in the previous week.

In Mexico, de Angoitia and Ramirez (2009) found that the cost-reduction strategy favoured by half the people they surveyed was to use their mobile phones strictly for incoming calls. This high-lights the importance of caller-pay systems, which allow users to receive calls for free and still have access to communication even when their credit has run out.

In countries where users are charged for incoming calls, they set limits on answering. Many avoid paying for phone time by simply turning off their phones, although the vast majority do this simply to conserve their phone batteries (Zainudeen and Iqbal 2008). However, Zainudeen and Iqbal warn that if this practice of using the phone mostly as a calling device becomes the norm, the prof-itability of the system will begin to degrade. "If widespread, this will reduce the efficiency of the network, where call attempts to switched-off phones cause costs but yield no revenue."

Despite the many strategies employed, few users take advantage of off-peak hour discounts. In Sri Lanka, 73% of mobile users do not phone on any particular day and 58% make no distinction regarding the time of day they make a call (Zainudeen and Iqbal 2008). The lack of uptake of off-peak discounts could be explained by the fact that in many countries, some people make or receive calls from their workplace or other people's homes. Thus, they may be choosing times based not on cost, but on what is most convenient for the friend or neighbour whose phone is being used, or for the person being called.

Zainudeen et al. (2010) elaborate on this:

> The real issue is whether these people have the opportunity to be "strategic" in their use. If callers (as well as the people they wish to call) only have access to a phone for a limited part of the day, and only at specific places, then they do not have the freedom to choose what kind of phone to use, where to use it, and how to use it, nor do they have the freedom to "mix and match" modes.

With the widespread use of prepaid phone time, more and more people have access to a phone. LIRNE*asia*'s 2011 Teleuse@BOP study showed that all users at the bottom of the pyramid in Bangladesh, India, and Java (Indonesia) were on prepaid subscriptions. In Sri Lanka and Thailand, the rates were 95% and 96% respectively. In a Mexican study, the figure was 92% (de Angoitia and Ramirez 2008). Although these rates have been hailed as a success, this group's failure to take advantage of off-peak discounts and monthly subscriptions means they may pay more for each phone call. It also means they may often have to resort to using their phone as a device to send simple signals, and then wait for someone to call them back.

Owners, borrowers, and renters

A 71-year-old West African man travelling to receive cancer treatment finds comfort in keeping in touch by mobile phone with his wife of 49 years. A Filipina mother receives word on her mobile phone from her daughter working in Saudi Arabia that the much-needed monthly remittance has been deposited in her account. Peruvian villagers, reeling from an earthquake, swiftly receive help from family members elsewhere because both sides own phones. Mobile phone ownership is helping out in numerous ways across the developing world.

In poor communities worldwide, phone ownership has exploded. A longitudinal study by LIRNE*asia* looked at rates of ownership among those at the bottom of the pyramid in six Asian countries

(Samarajiva 2011). It showed a marked increase in ownership between 2008 and 2011 and less reliance on other people's phones. In 2008, a third of the group owned their own phone, while the other two-thirds relied on the phones of other household members, friends and relatives, their workplace, or publicly accessible phones. By 2011, the ratio had reversed, with about two-thirds owning their own phone.

The greatest rise in phone ownership among the poor in that study was in Sri Lanka, where ownership rates went from 31% to 71% in three years (Samarajiva 2011). Bangladesh and Pakistan showed similar growth, while ownership in India remained stable: 36% in 2008 and 37% in 2011. Thailand's high ownership rate in 2008 (81%) rose further, to 88% in 2011. Meanwhile, in Latin America, ownership increased in just six years from less than a quarter of the population to almost nine out of every 10 citizens. According to DIRSI figures, ownership rose from 23% in 2003, to 55% in 2006, and 88% in 2009.

In 2007, 94% of all Jamaicans owned a mobile phone, while the number in Mexico stood at a mere 30% and in Argentina fell in the middle at 61% (Galperin and Mariscal 2007). Survey co-author Judith Mariscal described Latin America and the Caribbean as on two different planets with respect to mobile-phone ownership, with the large tourism industry in the Caribbean likely contributing to high ownership rates.

RIA survey results from 2011–2012 show that the uptake of mobile technology has also increased in Africa (Figure 6). Although the share of adults with mobile phones in Ethiopia (18%), Rwanda (24%), and Tanzania (36%) is still relatively low, these figures were up by about 15% in each case from 2007–2008. Meanwhile, Botswana and South Africa reached ownership levels of at least 80%. The researchers blame this disparity on the lack of competition in the low-ranking countries, as well as taxes that penalized the poor.

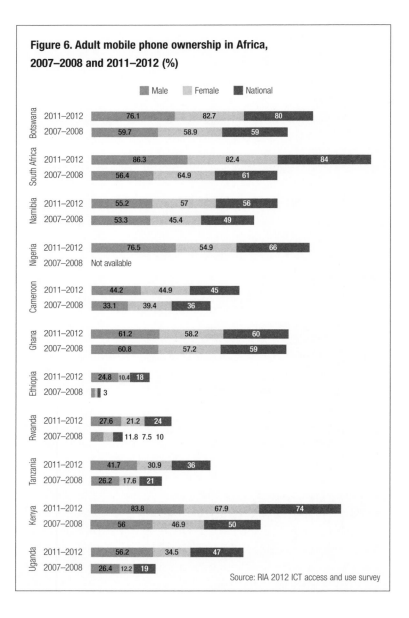

Figure 6. Adult mobile phone ownership in Africa, 2007–2008 and 2011–2012 (%)

Legend: ■ Male ■ Female ■ National

Botswana
2011–2012: 76.1 / 82.7 / 80
2007–2008: 59.7 / 58.9 / 59

South Africa
2011–2012: 86.3 / 82.4 / 84
2007–2008: 56.4 / 64.9 / 61

Namibia
2011–2012: 55.2 / 57 / 56
2007–2008: 53.3 / 45.4 / 49

Nigeria
2011–2012: 76.5 / 54.9 / 66
2007–2008: Not available

Cameroon
2011–2012: 44.2 / 44.9 / 45
2007–2008: 33.1 / 39.4 / 36

Ghana
2011–2012: 61.2 / 58.2 / 60
2007–2008: 60.8 / 57.2 / 59

Ethiopia
2011–2012: 24.8 / 10.4 / 18
2007–2008: 3

Rwanda
2011–2012: 27.6 / 21.2 / 24
2007–2008: 11.8 / 7.5 / 10

Tanzania
2011–2012: 41.7 / 30.9 / 36
2007–2008: 26.2 / 17.6 / 21

Kenya
2011–2012: 83.8 / 67.9 / 74
2007–2008: 56 / 46.9 / 50

Uganda
2011–2012: 56.2 / 34.5 / 47
2007–2008: 26.4 / 12.2 / 19

Source: RIA 2012 ICT access and use survey

Most people who don't own phones rely on either a household member or the family phone to make and receive calls, according to the LIRNE*asia* longitudinal study (Samarajiva 2011). In Asia, public phones and telecentres have always been other important points of access. In 2008, among the Bangladeshi and Indian poor who did not own a phone, 32% and 33% respectively used a public telephone. Three years later, with ownership rates on the rise, people relying on public phones dropped to 6% for Bangladesh and 8% for India. In Latin America, the cyber café continues to be an important public access point for the Internet, though this is changing as people increasingly go online through their mobile phone.

SIM cards are a popular alternative to owning a mobile phone. They are less costly than a phone and offer a greater sense of ownership than borrowing a phone. These memory chips, which can be inserted into other people's handsets, allow the user to keep a dedicated phone number and to store data, such as texting history and contacts' phone numbers.

"I don't have a mobile because I don't find it necessary. I have a fixed phone where I work, which I can use to make and receive calls."

— *Low-income focus group participant in an RIA study*

According to Herath (2008), borrowing phones from neighbours or friends is another common option in Asia for non-owners, and fixed-line phones are more likely to be shared than mobiles. He found that 31% of fixed-line and 7% of mobile owners allow non-family members to use their phone. (This could mean problems for borrowers as mobile phones begin to outnumber fixed-line phones in many countries.) In Africa, fixed phones are also more likely to be shared than mobiles, RIA found. In RIA's 2011–2012 survey, 68% of Africans said they do not share their mobile phone. Uganda fell well below that average, with only 41% of respondents saying they do not share their phones.

Renting time on someone else's phone appears to be fraught with difficulties (Zainudeen 2008). In Sri Lanka, 42% of survey respondents said they charge others for outgoing calls, while 19% of Indian respondents rented out their phones. What were renters' three top complaints? The phone was too far away (32%), charges were too high (24%), and there was no privacy (11%). According to Mariscal, the practice of renting appears to be unpopular in Latin America. In almost every country studied, owners did not rent out their phones. However, street resellers who deal in mobile minutes have been emerging in both Latin America and Africa. These entrepreneurs essentially act as mobile pay phones.

Public pay phones, telecentres, and village phones offer both advantages and disadvantages. Earlier, we saw that public pay phones or telecentres can save callers money when they were used in conjunction with mobile phone signals, but for many they lack privacy. "Sometimes, when you have five rand [60 cents Canadian], you would rather buy airtime because you want to discuss private matters, which cannot be discussed on a public phone," said a woman taking part in a rural focus group for an RIA study (Gillwald et al. 2010).

One sustainable shared system that does offer private lines appears to be the telephone cooperatives in Argentina. Established in the early 1960s as an offshoot of agricultural cooperatives, their many locations allow local groups to provide phone service to areas poorly served by the large operator ENTEL, which has tolerated their existence. The cooperatives now have more than 600,000 subscribers and account for 8% of the Argentine fixed-line market. Their presence is much greater in poor regions, such as the province of Jujuy, where they own 53% of installed lines. The cooperatives have led to savings, with average connection costs 32% lower than those charged by large operators. The cooperatives have kept up with technological changes and have eagerly entered the wireless market.

Grameen Village Phone: A pioneering innovation

The Grameen Village Phone program brought communications to millions of poor, rural Bangladeshis, while helping to stimulate local economies. It provided phone access to 45% of Bangladesh's villages and created thousands of entrepreneurs.

The program offered micro-loans to people deemed to have good credit by the phone company's banking arm, allowing them to buy a mobile phone. The phone owner then earned income by renting out time to neighbours. This not only increased phone access, but also provided a good living to many of the entrepreneurs.

One of the better-known success stories involves a woman named Begum. In 1997, the year the Grameen Village Phone program began, she became a "phone lady" (most of the operators were women), and the service she offered quickly became popular. Her growing monthly income allowed the former seamstress to buy property, including shops she would eventually run and houses she now rents out. She became the richest person in her village.

However, by 2007 the number of operators in the country had increased to more than 280,000. Handsets had become more affordable, and phone ladies were not earning the kind of money that would allow them to replicate Begum's success. A Grameen Telecom spokesperson acknowledged that, 10 years after the program began, the average operator was earning an annual income of only $70. However, the Grameen Village Phone program was an important stopgap in the era before mobile phone ownership became more of a reality for rural Bangladeshis. It also proved to telecommunications companies that rural residents were a viable market. The model has been exported to Africa, with a similar service now operating in rural Uganda and Rwanda.

Sources: Knight-John 2008, Shaffer 2007, and Grameen Foundation promotional literature

Radio and TV retain an important role in Africa

Radio is the communications device that Africans use most. The tremendous growth in mobile phone use and high demand for the Internet belie the fact that most Africans turn to the radio for news, information, and entertainment. On a continent where TV coverage is sparse and access is usually limited to free, state-run broadcasters, a survey of 17 countries revealed large numbers of radio listeners — so many that they outnumber mobile phone owners.

RIA's 2007–2008 study found that 90% of Senegalese and 88% of Ghanaians listen to radio, while 87% of Ugandans and 89% of Zambians and Mozambicans over the age of 16 own their own radio. During the same period, the number of mobile phone or SIM card owners among those over age 16 ranged from 21% in Uganda to 60% in Ghana. However, mobile ownership is clearly on the rise, whereas radio ownership is stagnating. The cost of batteries is a key factor in radio listening time. "Although radio is the most commonly used ICT, financial resources to buy batteries play a great part in determining whether a person can afford to listen to the radio or not" (Gillwald et al. 2010).

Radio appears to be less dominant in Asia and Latin America. In India, the phone has overtaken radio as an important household item. One study found that out of 100 Indian homes at the bottom of the socio-economic pyramid, 50 had TVs, 38 had phones, 28 had radios, and one had a computer. In Pakistan, many tune in to radio via their mobile phone, with 7% listening to radio stations on their handsets, according to LIRNE*asia*.

In Latin America, radio is one of the least preferred media for advertising. In a recent survey of Mexican businesses, it was preferred by only 2.2% of respondents, whereas the Internet was the first choice for 8.8%. Ironically, the loudspeaker (far from a high-tech device) was the advertising medium chosen by most (22%). Despite its unpopularity with advertisers, radio broadcasting remains an important local medium in Mexico: 80% of survey respondents without a community radio station said it was very important that one be built in their town.

Research on television use in some African countries highlights interesting gender issues. For example, men prefer to watch television outside the home, typically taking in televised sports events with other men in a bar (Gillwald et al. 2010). Many women complain that if they watch television in public, they will be subject to undue scrutiny. "The culture won't let me go out, order a drink and watch TV," said one woman interviewed in the study. Despite the stigma, a growing number of African women have been trying to break the taboo. However, others say that going out to watch television squanders scarce resources and they prefer to use that money to supplement meagre food budgets.

Why the poor use ICTs

The mobile revolution explained

How did so many people of very limited means gain access to mobile technology in such a short time? LIRNE*asia* explains the sequence of events:

> *Voice connectivity was achieved for a majority of the world's people, including substantial numbers of the poor, because governments removed or lowered barriers to participation in the supply of telecom services and created conditions conducive to competition, even if that competition was less than perfect. This was the necessary condition. Where multiple suppliers existed, intense competition occurred — the critical step in implementing the budget telecom network model. The radically lower prices attracted more minutes of use, which, in turn, made further reductions possible. Operators were able to load their networks with high volumes of revenue-yielding minutes because they*

had succeeded in reducing the transaction costs of dealing with large numbers of customers who generate small amounts of revenue. Prepaid, which reduces transaction costs and also accommodates the needs of those with irregular earning patterns, was a critical element. (Samarajiva 2010)

Many others have also credited the prepaid system with playing a key role in this new phone ubiquity. Bonina and Illa (2008) describe the advantages it offers the poor and the telecommunications companies serving them:

These advantages include the relatively low costs incurred by users for starting up mobile phone service (activation of the line, SIM card, equipment, etc.), and the possibility of controlling expenses and not being required to sign a contract, which means the user does not have to prove that he or she can qualify for a loan, which is extremely difficult in countries where economic instability and recurring crisis make lines of credit scarce in general. The prepaid system, meanwhile, has benefits for the operator, who does not have to send monthly statements of charges and avoids the risk of users defaulting on contract payments.

Mobile phones have become more affordable to own and take less time to install than fixed-line phones. People have often had to wait years for fixed lines to reach their towns. Phone access no longer means signing up for long-term subscriptions, which has always shut out those with sporadic incomes. For non-owners, mobile phones are easier to borrow (or rent time on) now that more friends, relatives, and neighbours own them. For those with low incomes, a virtuous circle appears to have been achieved, as improved access to the phone gives users more opportunities to make and receive calls, which inevitably increases phone activity, further integrating the phone into their lives.

Help in a crisis

When someone with a low income makes a call on a mobile phone, they are likely calling a friend or relative. The DIRSI researchers who interviewed 7,000 people from poor households in Latin America and the Caribbean add weight to this assertion (Galperin and Mariscal 2007). More than two-thirds of their interviewees' calls were to friends and family. Meanwhile, RIA's 2007–2008 household and individual survey found that business calls constituted, on average, only 8% of mobile phone calls.

Although people with low incomes use phones mainly for social calls, potential emergencies consistently rank high on surveys as the reason for buying a phone or the perceived need for one. According to LIRNE*asia*, this is because many developing countries lack the standard emergency services found in developed countries. In the absence of such a service, people call a family member or a friend for help in a crisis.

Better than lighting fires or reading coca leaves

In 2007, Alterna Perú interviewed residents of Canas, a remote province in the Peruvian highlands (Alterna Perú 2008). The province had signed an agreement with a large operator the previous year, which resulted in widespread adoption of mobile and fixed wireless phones. Before then, people in the area had little access to telecommunications. Interviewees described how mobile phones had changed several aspects of life in Canas, including their ability to deal with emergencies.

> Before the mobile phone, we communicated in the hills with whistles, lanterns, or when there were big problems we lit fires to indicate a serious problem and the people, seeing that, came to help.
>
> — *Pedro Ramos, former president of a "rondas," or peasant-policing group, in the town of Yanaoca*

> The animals got lost and [my son] fell in the mountain and could not get up. Thanks to the mobile phone he told me that he was lying in the mountain and asked me to pick him up [which I did]. Before, I would have had to read coca leaves to guess where he was.
>
> — *Hermenegildo Choqque, father of a cattle herder*

The social currency of ICTs

The convenience of picking up a handset and the speed of a phone call or text message sometimes can mean the difference between life and death, health and illness, prosperity and poverty, or democracy and dictatorship. The following examples illustrate how ICTs have made a difference in the lives of the poor.

Health: In South Africa, tuberculosis patients receive mobile phone messages reminding them to take their medication at specific times. This results in compliance rates similar to those recorded when patients attend the clinic and are observed taking their medicine, but is achieved at a lower cost. In another case, an impact study by the Indian Space Research Organisation showed how providing satellite-based telemedicine in remote areas can decrease patient costs by 81%, thanks to the reduced need for travel, accommodation, and treatment at hospitals. Finally, a cost–benefit study of the use of smartphones in the surveillance of disease incidence in rural Uganda found that the Ministry of Health could save significant financial and medical resources if the program was rolled out across the whole country.

Education: An IDRC-supported study sought to explore the use of short message service (SMS) for non-formal education. Researchers in the Philippines made SMS-based learning modules available to a cohort of out-of-school youth and adult learners. Most of the students welcomed the idea of learning through text messages and were willing to set aside a portion of their prepaid credits to learn by using their phone. Mean test scores of those in the SMS group were marginally higher than those in a control group that did not use SMS-based learning modules.

Another project sought to understand how mobile phone games could improve English-language skills among children from rural, low-income families in India. In an after-school program, a pilot project used mobile phone games to target spelling, word recognition, listening comprehension, and sentence construction.

Pre- and post-intervention assessments revealed an improvement in spelling test results, with the average score increasing after the mobile intervention from 5.2 to 8.4 out of 18.

Political empowerment: Much anecdotal and qualitative evidence attests to the role of technology in facilitating collective action. The toppling in 2001 of the president of the Philippines, Joseph Estrada, is often cited as an example of how technology brought down a government, with SMS-organized street rallies and online accounts of his impeachment trial. President Gloria Macapagal-Arroyo, who directly benefited from this "e-coup," was also subject to cyber scandal when her taped conversation with an election official became the most popular ring tone on mobile phones in the country. The fuelling of Arab Spring uprisings by ICTs provided evidence that the growing prevalence of mobiles and the Internet is having a greater impact on political action than ever before. Whether technology is inherently democratic (as "liberation technologists" argue) or simply amplifies existing political movements, including harmful ones, is still open to question.

Businesses that benefit

Saving time and money on transportation has emerged as the greatest economic benefit of mobile phone ownership, according to a LIRNE*asia* study. In the developing world, stories abound of people using their phone to complete a business task that would normally have required travel. Sixto Chino, a T-shirt and jacket manufacturer in Peru, provides a good illustration of this (Alterna Perú 2008). Without a telephone, he would have to leave his business in the afternoon, travel overnight, spend the next day buying the goods he needs, and then return home that night. Thanks to the phone, he now calls in his orders and only travels to a nearby town to pick up the shipment. The change has reduced his expenses by half.

Alterna Perú (2008) uncovered many economic benefits that the mobile phone brings to the working poor and residents of isolated areas. During interviews the group conducted in the province of Canas, several business people spoke about changes brought about by their newly acquired mobile phones. Cattle ranchers could contact veterinarians more easily when one of their animals was distressed or ill. That has helped reduce mortality among their livestock and significantly increased meat and milk production. Phones have allowed many small business owners to sell their goods to buyers in other districts, thus expanding their network of customers and increasing revenues.

For many, the phone has simply become a time saver, allowing them to get quotes on the materials they need, for example. For machinery dealer Jacinto Ramos, the ability to call his suppliers has allowed him to calculate his costs more accurately. "Before the mobile phone, we had to queue up [at the public phone], call some relative and tell him to go to the hardware store and ask. It was not direct. Sometimes it went well, sometimes it did not."

In Bihar, India, beautician Poonam Devi provides an example of how small entrepreneurs have discovered the economic benefits of owning a mobile phone. Devi, who earns the equivalent of US$40 a month, credits her phone for her rising income. Much of her work is now done by phone: ordering beauty supplies and receiving calls from customers who want to make an appointment. "I know everybody, and everybody knows me as a beautician."

Mobile money for the "unbanked"

Many people in developing countries have no bank account. In Latin America, for example, only 14.5% of poor households had a savings account in 2006 (Mariscal 2009). Access to banking can help the poor during periods of unemployment or ill-health, but many remain without those services.

According to RIA's Christoph Stork (2012), banks offer few incentives for the poor to deposit their savings. "You are being

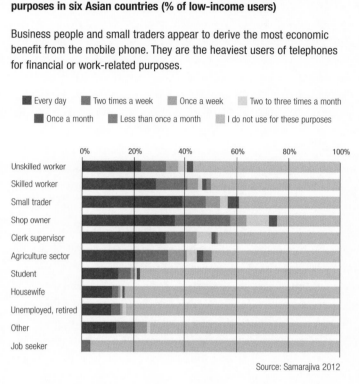

Figure 7. Use of the telephone for financial, business, or work-related purposes in six Asian countries (% of low-income users)

Business people and small traders appear to derive the most economic benefit from the mobile phone. They are the heaviest users of telephones for financial or work-related purposes.

■ Every day   ■ Two times a week   ■ Once a week   Two to three times a month
■ Once a month   ■ Less than once a month   ■ I do not use for these purposes

Unskilled worker
Skilled worker
Small trader
Shop owner
Clerk supervisor
Agriculture sector
Student
Housewife
Unemployed, retired
Other
Job seeker

0%   20%   40%   60%   80%   100%

Source: Samarajiva 2012

On the web | THE RESEARCH

charged for depositing money into an account, you're being charged for withdrawing money from an account, and you're being charged for transferring the account, so why on earth do you want to put it into the account?" he asked during a panel session at the ICTD2012 conference in Atlanta, Georgia. On top of that, many of the poor do not have a home address or the documents required to open an account, or a bank located anywhere near their homes or businesses.

As many more poor people have access to a phone than to a bank, "mobile money" has gained in popularity. This system entails a consumer sending a payment request via a text message, after which a charge is applied to their phone bill or their online wallet. The merchant involved is immediately informed of the successful payment and releases the goods. Advocates say it suits the needs of the poor better than conventional banking. According to Mariscal (2009), mobile money can address the two key barriers to financial inclusion for those without a bank account: affordability and physical availability. With global remittances exceeding US$400 billion in 2012 (World Bank 2013), not to mention domestic money transfers, those at the bottom of the income pyramid are an important market, and many players now offer mobile money services.

In 2011, RIA researchers surveyed 1,200 Ugandan households. In a paper published the following year, RIA's Christoph Stork wrote that 13.9% used mobile money and just under half owned a mobile phone. The survey subjects found that mobile money was faster, easier, and safer than conventional methods, and that convenience and cost were the next most popular reasons for using it. The research team also surveyed 500 businesses, most of them informal: 68% used mobile phones and 17% used mobile money, mainly to receive payments or to pay suppliers.

Stork has devised a model that would make transactions free, with operators benefiting from access to large amounts of capital. However, this model calls for regulatory agencies and policymakers to make some big changes to the system. Meanwhile, DIRSI's Judith Mariscal recommends more clarity in the requirements to become a mobile money agent and better consumer protection before mobile money will truly benefit the poor.

Phone-related jobs

The mobile phone industry has generated many jobs that serve the sector. The obvious ones are those held by the employees of telecommunications companies. Others are in the mining sector, particularly in Africa, where materials needed for the manufacture of phones are extracted: for example, gold, tantalum, tin, tungsten, and cobalt.

Some lesser-known jobs have come about thanks to the entrepreneurial spirit that often accompanies the introduction of new technology. People repair phones; sell airtime, SIM cards, and batteries; or set up recharging posts in bars or beside busy roads. In Africa, one entrepreneur builds smartphones for those who can't afford advanced features. This person removes and resells the circuitry from high-end phones, providing the status-conscious, lower-income customer with what appears to be an expensive phone, but one that simply calls and texts.

Online and on the job

The Internet's low numbers in the developing world, especially when accessed through a personal computer, do not take away from the fact that it has helped many small businesses thrive. In Namibia, for example, Patience Smith interviewed small business owners who had benefited from the Internet:

➤ Renate, 50, works from home as a consultant, preparing visa and passport applications. Through her home computer, she keeps in touch with her agency by email (she also uses a mobile phone), downloading and printing government applications.

➤ Anastasia, 35, owns a Namibian restaurant and guesthouse called The Farmhouse. A website helped her business achieve international recognition, and she also earns income from an Internet café.

On the web
THE RESEARCH

→ Zelda, 32, owns a hair salon, a manicure operation, and a beauty products outlet. She records client information and follows up with email to gauge satisfaction. All three stores are located in the same shopping centre, and their employees often refer clients to one another through email.

Price alerts for farmers

Good information is like rich soil to the farmer. From the cost of seed and fertilizer to weather conditions and market prices, the right information can make the difference between profitability and poverty for farmers in developing countries. According to LIRNE*asia* (Lokanathan et al. 2011), getting that information has been time-consuming for many small farmers. And of every $5 a farmer spends to sell produce, $1 goes toward finding the information needed to make the sale.

LIRNE*asia* researchers have been following the mobile application initiatives that have allowed farmers and agricultural traders to become better informed. The largest mobile operator in Sri Lanka, Dialog Axiata, with initial help from LIRNE*asia*, has been providing market information through a price-alert system to farmers whose produce is ready for sale. The system, called Tradenet, matches buyers and sellers, and allows farmers to profit by timing a trip to the market based on price information.

For example, a smallholder Sri Lankan farmer, growing onions, cabbage, and a few other crops on little more than half a hectare, was able to use the information he obtained through his Tradenet subscription to benefit from a large fluctuation in cabbage prices. As he was preparing to harvest his crop, he noticed the per-kilogram price of cabbage rise from 18 cents (US$) in the morning to 32 cents by the end of the day. On the strength of that upward trend, he enlisted family and friends to help him quickly harvest the crop overnight. The next day, he sold his cabbages at the market for 41 cents a kilo, 35% higher than the average price.

ICT solutions for the pineapple farmer

Pineapples are in high demand, both by local hotels that serve them to their guests and international buyers who ship them around the world. Yet, many pineapple growers in the developing world struggle to produce fruit that meets the high standards expected. Farmers are faced with several challenges: finding land to grow their saplings, identifying the saplings that will produce high-quality fruit, acquiring the specialized knowledge needed for a successful yield, and realizing an adequate financial return on their efforts in a market where prices fluctuate. Galpaya (2012) described these problems and suggested how the ICT community could provide solutions. (Volunteers at Random Hacks of Kindness have done some preliminary work on developing useful applications for pineapple growers.)

Problem	Possible solution
Pineapple growers can't find enough land, often due to misconceptions by landowners that pineapples leave the soil nutrient-poor.	Develop a system that matches landowners and farmers, while disseminating authoritative soil information.
It's difficult to tell if a sapling will turn into a good-quality pineapple plant.	Have farmers rank saplings. After using a supplier, they rate the product, texting the information to a collection point, where the rankings are then made available to all farmers.
Many farmers lack the specialized knowledge needed to grow a good pineapple.	Through a simple networking system, establish an on-demand advice service provided by peers who are experienced farmers.
Many growers are unaware of the fluctuations in the market and miss out on opportunities.	Build a platform for spot and futures trading, as well as a simple eBay-like system for buyers and sellers to find each other.

Living mobile

Law students use their mobile phones to look up case law and avoid standing in line for a computer at their university. Drivers use their phones to let others know where they saw a police cruiser hiding. One church volunteer consults the clock on a mobile phone before ringing the church bell. The mobile phone has become a convenient part of daily life across the developing world.

At the same time, ICTs, and particularly mobile phones, have been at the forefront in collecting health data, tracking hotspots of violence, and finding earthquake victims. Applications have helped monitor elections and track medical supplies. One phone call can make a big difference in someone's day, while a single picture sent from a mobile phone can spark a social movement.

The group Alterna Perú (2008) looked at the impact of mobile phones on several industries and social agencies in Canas. This region is home to many cattle breeders, and the study found considerable increases in productivity directly related to use of the mobile phone for veterinary emergencies and artificial insemination of cows. It also found that the mobile phone helped businesses expand beyond their provincial boundaries and save time in obtaining materials.

However, enthusiasm over this new access can sometimes drown out other voices, as researchers question what all this new technology does to traditional life. "Sometimes, the positive benefits are counterbalanced by the emergence of new behaviours," write Smith et al. (2011). Although they claim that mobile phones constitute the basis for one of the greatest expansions of human capabilities in history, the authors remind us that the technology has also been used to fan civil violence and that "mobile access may create the 'unfreedom' associated with the expectations of always being online."

New jobs and new social opportunities have arisen with the new technologies. It is ironic, however, that some people who can fix a computer or sell airtime cannot afford to browse the Internet or have a conversation on a friend's mobile phone. Some others feel that calling a client by mobile phone is just too expensive, and that a face-to-face conversation will suffice.

Can ICT access help ease poverty?

Building social capital

IDRC-supported researchers who have sought to understand and measure the extent to which ICTs play a role in reducing poverty have uncovered some evidence that connects ICTs and poverty alleviation.

Many researchers in the ICT for development field believe that improving people's ability to communicate can lead to improved socio-economic conditions. Many have seen first-hand how being able to contact a neighbour by phone or a friend by Skype helps maintain relationships and deepen a sense of belonging. As social connections often lead to job opportunities, especially in the developing world, gaining "social capital" improves the ability to make a living. As PICTURE Africa's Kathleen Diga (2013) points out, "In poor settings, social relationships are intrinsically linked to economic issues; people usually get jobs or loans from family and friends."

A mobile phone may lead directly to employment. A job hopeful with a mobile phone number can be reached more easily than someone who doesn't own a phone or depends on someone else's. Income can also result from sources other than employment. For example, a phone helps solidify relationships with far-flung family members who may be in a position to send remittances home. Those remittances, in turn, can help pay for more phone calls to those family members, increasing both the contact and the potential for continued support.

Social capital plays an important role in bringing in money for the very poor. The access that allows the poor to earn that social capital requires certain actions from authorities: for example, regulatory changes that promote competition and lower ICT costs. Thus, a key challenge in improving ICT access lies in

On the web
THE RESEARCH

convincing governments to make the policy and regulatory changes that encourage investment in technology and access that will ultimately help the poorest.

ICT access and the way out of extreme poverty

Some of the strongest evidence that ICTs can help alleviate poverty has emerged from PICTURE Africa. Researchers undertook a seminal study that shows a link between ICT access and a rise in income levels among the very poor (May et al. n.d.). In a survey of 1,600 East African households in 2007 and again in 2010, they found that the very poor with access to ICTs were able to spend US$21 more a month than those without access. The gains added 0.5% to annual household income and narrowed the gap between those earning the least income and others in higher-income brackets. People at the bottom of the income pyramid who lacked access to ICTs did not move up from the poorest category.

The study provides evidence of a relationship between a rise in income for the very poor and access to ICTs. "The finding is significant because it shows that a mobile phone on its own leads to an increase in income," Julian May told South Africa's *Mail & Guardian* (Cooke 2012). Moreover, he added, "If you put a mobile phone into the hands of someone with an additional year of education, their income increased further, and if you add skills and entrepreneurship training, this income figure increases even more."

An IDRC internal report concludes: "ICTs do make a difference to the livelihoods of the poor and do contribute toward reducing both financial and non-financial dimensions of poverty. The availability of mobile phones in particular is, therefore, a potentially valuable tool to improve the livelihood of the very poor over the medium term."

The study took place during a time of dramatic increases in the price of food. According to May, "access to ICT buffered people against poverty" (Cooke 2012). In the same study, the authors calculated that an increase in income results in a much greater chance of gaining access to ICTs. An additional year of education also improves that chance by about 30% (May et al. n.d.).

UN Secretary-General Ban Ki-moon has recognized the significance of the study's findings. In his 2012 report on poverty eradication, he referred to PICTURE Africa's research as showing that getting ICTs into the hands of the poor can make a difference.

> *Access to those technologies is increasingly recognized as an important means of improving the situation of excluded groups by reducing poverty, improving health and mitigating the impact of geographical isolation. A recent study in East Africa found that access to such technologies, particularly mobile phones and the Internet, helped to reduce poverty among the poorest populations (Ban Ki-moon 2012).*

Another study from PICTURE Africa, conducted in two villages in Tanzania, also linked ICT investment with poverty alleviation (Diga, 2013). Residents of one village received five months of mobile phone airtime and Internet access, while the other villagers received no ICTs. The first village experienced a reduction in all seven of the poverty criteria used. In the second village, changes were seen in only two of the indicators.

In Latin America, a 2010 DIRSI study followed a large cohort of Peruvians who became Internet users between 2007 and 2009 and compared them with non-users in the same period (De Los Ríos, 2010). The household incomes of Internet users were 19% higher, on average, than those who remained non-users. The effect was larger in rural than in urban areas. Higher incomes were also associated with frequency of use. In a more recent study in Ecuador, DIRSI researchers found that after introducing broadband services in a municipality, individual labour income rose on average by 7.5% (Katz and Callorda 2013).

On the web
THE RESEARCH

Nigeria spends a billion dollars a year on ICTs

"In a developing and emerging market like Nigeria, that is quite a large amount of money," said Omobola Johnson, the country's minister of communication technology, referring to the billion dollars her government now spends annually on ICTs. Speaking at the ICTD2012 conference in Atlanta, Georgia, she outlined how the government is diversifying what is primarily a resource-based economy and working toward the goal of making Nigeria a top 20 economy by 2020.

It plans to lay down 15,000 kilometres of fibre-optic cable in urban and commercial areas, ensuring connectivity for the tertiary sector and building hundreds of government websites to improve online services. The private telecommunications industry is also involved, with an increased focus on underserved areas. Nigeria is operating on the premise that, in addition to investment in basic needs, spending on communications is needed to bring the 90% of the population who live on $2 a day or less out of poverty.

Part 4

Lessons for policymakers

ICTs play a positive role in poverty alleviation

In earlier chapters, we introduced the idea of ICTs as development tools and described how IDRC-funded researchers have uncovered links between ICTs and poverty. Research results, both qualitative and quantitative, have shown how and why those at the bottom of the income pyramid use communication tools. They also highlight connections between access to technology and poverty alleviation.

If key impediments to greater access to ICTs by the poor are availability and cost, what steps should policymakers take to ensure that ICTs are available and affordable? Does Internet access have to be at broadband speeds? Why is collecting information on how the poor use ICTs important for achieving access goals?

On the web
THE LESSONS

"The quickest way to get out of poverty right now is to have a mobile phone," Grameen Bank founder Muhammad Yunus told an IDRC-sponsored Harvard Forum on ICTs and poverty in 2003. ICTs, such as the mobile phone, offset the ill-effects of poverty in many ways. They help connect people in times of need, play a role in increasing productivity, and ensure greater access to information. However, if the link between ICT use and poverty alleviation is more clearly established, how can we ensure that the poor get access to ICTs? The following are a few important lessons that researchers from Latin America, Africa, and Asia have learned about how government, civil society, and the private sector can all play a role in ensuring greater inclusion in the benefits of ICT access.

The case for breaking up monopolies

In much of Latin America, two large telecommunications operators maintain a duopoly, with few able to challenge their domination of the market. As in any market that discourages competition, Latin America has the highest average mobile phone and Internet subscription costs in the world. Governments, such as Brazil's, favour high costs, as almost half of mobile broadband fees go to taxes. DIRSI has often argued that lowering taxes on ICTs is critical. However, the consensus among ICT for development experts is that telecommunications markets must be opened to competition if prices are to come down.

In the 1990s, several Latin American countries looked to the example set by the United States, where the AT&T behemoth was divided into eight different companies. Brazil, similarly, broke up its largest company into several components. Chile, which has a strong regulator, also agreed that a new competitive environment was necessary. Mexico, which for many years lacked the political will to take on the dominant Telmex, is now welcoming new telecommunications players.

Africa, meanwhile, has seen widespread privatization. However, the state has generally retained a controlling share and provided ongoing protection of the dominant company at the expense of new entrants into the emerging competitive markets. In South Africa, Telkom SA was forced to pay a maximum fine after a series of complaints of anti-competitiveness against it, which arose from its private monopoly period.

Competition comes from start-ups

If governments want to create healthy competition, issuing new licences to telecommunications players is the most readily available intervention. The governments of South Asia have awarded numerous mobile licences. This has transformed the region into one of the most affordable places on earth to talk on a mobile phone. Several South Asian countries offer a standard bundle of telecommunications services for the equivalent of less than US$5 a month.

Large existing companies are often resistant to the licensing of new entrants into the market. Groups such as LIRNE*asia*, DIRSI, and RIA can make a difference by providing evidence to governments of the benefits of competition.

New entrants bring lower prices and introduce new ways of doing business — a situation referred to as "disruptive innovation" (a term coined by Harvard Business School professor Clayton Christensen). In East Africa, for example, a small player introduced a new service that allowed clients to roam for a signal in a neighbouring country but to be charged at their home-country rate. That move compelled the three dominant operators in the region to offer the same service, with inexpensive roaming capability eventually becoming widespread not only in East Africa but also across the continent.

Although the affordability of mobiles and the Internet in most
South Asian and several African countries can be linked to
increased competition in those countries, something else is also
at play: the business model of low-fee operators. They target low-
income customers, tend to keep transaction costs low, and load
large numbers of customers on each network so that their businesses remain financially viable. They are to the telecommunications industry what Ireland's Ryanair is to the airline industry:
no-frills, low-cost service providers, where revenues are based
on large numbers of low-margin sales.

Important data must be released

For many researchers trying to understand ICT use at the bottom
of the socio-economic pyramid, obtaining data remains a challenge. Telecommunications operators have the best information
on ICT use — more than governments, regulators, and researchers.
However, they tend to keep information private, usually for commercial reasons. Their reluctance to release information on ICT
use leads to large discrepancies in estimates of broadband coverage. For example, in Mexico, the principal telecommunications
operator claims more than 90% coverage, while the industry regulator has found it to be only 65%. With this kind of confusion,
the regulatory authorities have difficulty judging whether the
company is fulfilling its obligation to extend its network to
underserved areas where most of the poor live.

Regulatory authorities need a stronger hand in demanding information that would provide a clearer picture and help researchers
better understand the connection between ICT access and poverty
alleviation. However, even those with the authority to demand
such information come up against recalcitrant companies. In
South Africa, for example, regulators are stymied by the country's
telecommunications operators, who refuse to comply with
demands for information. The regulators cannot afford to use

their already scarce funds to take the fight any further. Ironically, Kenya, whose regulatory agency has fewer legal "teeth" than South Africa's, appears to be more successful in obtaining this information.

While telecommunications operators hold valuable information, many government departments also keep vital public data out of reach of potential users. LIRNE*asia* sees many young people keen to develop mobile applications in response to consumer demand, but government departments, not understanding the value of their data, inadvertently impede improvements in the sector.

Whether generated by the private sector or collected in government departments, information on ICT use can help researchers understand how to use technology to improve the social conditions of those at the bottom of the pyramid. More data can also give programmers and designers the key bits of information they need to build socially relevant technological innovations.

Information is also essential for informing government decisions, as demonstrated in Sri Lanka and Bangladesh. In both these countries, governments had proposed a change in how mobile phone communications were taxed. LIRNE*asia*'s data on the amount the poor spend on mobile communications helped make the point that these new taxes would disproportionately hurt that segment of the population. In light of this information, both governments modified the tax.

While researchers try to obtain more data, they are also trying to take specific communities into account. Otherwise, huge differences among user groups may be obliterated by aggregated statistics. They also want to see proper benchmarks established, so that data can be compared among countries. This makes collaborative efforts such as the Observatory for the Information Society in Latin America and the Caribbean that much more vital.

Governments' role in increasing ICT access

Some researchers believe that the best way for governments to be involved in increasing ICT access is to focus on economic regulation, reforming markets to make them more competitive, and continuing to work on underlying democratic tenets that allow a fair and competitive environment to flourish. Governments can also set up policy processes that are public and participatory.

Rather than employing the traditional arms of government, such as ministries or departments of industry or technology, governments appear to want to increase investments in technology through their departments of education. Across Latin America, the One Laptop per Child initiative has been promoted aggressively, with mixed results.

In Brazil, another large-scale government education initiative aims to connect 60,000 schools to the Internet. The agreement for this project was the result of a swap. The incumbent telecommunications operators had a contractual obligation to use a "universal access fund" to provide public telephones. However, in the era of the increasingly popular mobile phone, public facilities were no longer needed. Instead, the company agreed to use the funds to install an Internet connection in every school in the country.

A great challenge, however, is the lack of clear evidence to justify these decisions. Although a few small research studies point to ICTs' positive influence on educational outcomes, others show little impact on learning.

Education departments can play a vital role in training people in basic computer literacy and the skills needed to fulfill job requirements. A traditional government tool, the telecentre, continues to be an important training venue for a host of skills, even though it has lost some ground to the individual use of mobile phones.

The ICT sector can also benefit from government funding for its infrastructure. In Argentina and Brazil, new public operators were set up to deploy and operate backbone networks. They provide wholesale connectivity to local private operators, something that usually benefits citizens living in least-served areas. This move has likely been the catalyst for a price drop of about 45% between 2010 and 2012 for broadband services in Brazil. Several African countries have dealt with their broadband deficit by entering into long-term agreements with equipment supply companies, such as Huawei in Uganda, to build their network.

Although government spending on infrastructure has worked in some jurisdictions, in many cases politicians and bureaucrats have failed in their efforts to take an active role in the industry. In one African country, for example, a department took so long to implement its project to sell wholesale broadband to private operators that, during the three-year lag, the private companies built the needed infrastructure themselves. Those were important years in terms of changes in the telecommunications industry, with a growing need for more wireless capacity, and the private companies realized it was best for them to go it alone.

Many feel that the best thing governments can do to promote ICT access is to get out of the way. India has succeeded in the information technology sphere mainly because the government has not interfered. Innovation often happens in decentralized ways, not top-down or emanating from a central entity like government. Governments need to make sure decentralized innovation takes place. They may provide encouragement by creating incubators, fostering interactions among entrepreneurs, and encouraging investors to come on board.

Getting out of the way also means not pricing the poor out of the market by taxing individual phone calls. And it means categorizing communication services as a vital need for society, rather than as a luxury. Bhutan offers a good lesson in how government can avoid taxing phone calls but still find funding for the rural poor. The government there held an auction for a second mobile licence — then put the large proceeds of the sale back into making service available to those who were not served by either operator.

Governments should also avoid too much prognostication, as they seem to have a bad track record in predicting the popularity of a service or the scalability of a technological innovation. In the early days of mobile phone service, many developing-country governments viewed it as something for the rich, meanwhile subsidizing fixed-line telephony for the poor and using universal service fees to help fund their installation in rural areas. These schemes operated at a lumbering pace. Meanwhile, the mobile industry aimed its products at all sectors and grew at lightning speed.

The Internet needs an ecosystem

Just as potential users of voice telephony must learn how to make and receive calls, in the case of the Internet, literacy and the ability to navigate complex interfaces are required. Interfaces have become much simpler with the transition from conventional computers to tablets and smartphones. In the future, voice recognition might simplify use even further. Adoption of the Internet, therefore, depends on the existence of an ecosystem that includes users with the necessary skills, devices, infrastructure, and, most important, applications and content that users want.

Content is king

Broadband access to the Internet must be viewed as part of an ecosystem that touches all aspects of life. But it is not the big pipes and wireless devices that will educate children, give people jobs, and build communities. The physical infrastructure is only one part of a system that includes popular platforms and vital applications — in short, good content. It is not technology itself that spurs change, but what people do with it.

Governments putting together ICT plans must think beyond just providing the technology. They have to encourage and enable people to build popular and useful content. And they should avoid altering cost structures that could imperil popular platforms, such as Facebook and YouTube — the vehicles that engage so many people and make them familiar with the Internet.

Regions differ

Although one aim of this book has been to bring together best practices from various regions, global approaches are not always the answer. Sometimes issues are culturally specific and may be dealt with very differently from one country or region to another. Other factors, such as cost, must also be considered. E-education and e-health projects may be a viable solution in one country, but too costly for another. There are no one-size-fits-all policy and regulatory responses. Much can be learned from the experience of others, but, in all cases, solutions must be adapted to local conditions if they are to succeed.

On the web
THE LESSONS

Part 5

The future

Throughout this book, we have seen the roles that the Internet and mobile phones play in the lives of the poor — how ICTs can give people a sense of belonging in their communities, provide them with information from beyond their communities, and often help them earn a better living. However, although technology has been an economic boon to the poor and other marginalized groups, it also threatens to diminish their power. As a result, new opportunities and challenges of this increasingly networked world must be regularly assessed.

The open movement offers promise

Several open initiatives have increased civil democracy on the Internet, as well as opportunities for learning, scientific collaboration, and free enterprise. Many hope that disenfranchised, threatened, and vulnerable groups will discover opportunities in the open movement's various guises.

On the web
THE LESSONS

- **Open government** is more transparent, accessible, and responsive. Its advocates call for more freely available and reusable online data in areas such as health, education, procurement, and transport. The availability of such data promises to lead to a more informed citizenry and increased opportunities. BudgIT, for example, is a Nigerian start-up that uses open budget data to retell the Nigerian budget and public data in finer detail across every literacy level. It aims to stimulate citizen interest around public data and trigger discussions about better governance.

- **Open learning** calls for educational resources to be freely shared on the Internet. So far, initiatives such as Khan Academy and MIT's OpenCourseWare have proved immensely popular. They have already delivered hundreds of millions of courses to hundreds of millions of people around the world.

- **Open science** tries to make scientific research more publicly available, providing data and findings for free reuse. It also encourages transparency in how research is conducted and promotes the use of Web-based tools to facilitate scientific collaboration. The Galaxy Zoo project, for example, allowed more than 200,000 volunteers to classify galaxies by examining images online, leading to more than 150 million new classifications.

- **Open business models** enable entrepreneurs to generate revenue through free and openly licensed content. One example is technobrega in Belém, Brazil, where artists forego traditional copyright and willingly share their creations with informal street vendors. The vendors market and distribute the music and help to increase the artists' popularity. Significant revenues are then realized through paid events, such as popular dance parties.

Harnessing the crowd

Crowdsourcing — which assigns tasks to an undefined, large group of people or communities — has been catching on with entrepreneurs and activists, who have increasingly been appealing to the owners of mobile devices.

Platforms such as Ushahidi illustrate how open calls can elicit a response to humanitarian crises, corruption, or electoral fraud. Initially developed to help map reports of violence in Kenya after the 2008 post-election fallout, Ushahidi allows anyone to gather distributed data via text message, email, or the Internet and turn it into a visual image, such as a timeline or map. At the time of publication, this open-source platform had been adopted and deployed more than 12,000 times across the world for a wide variety of problems, including tracking sexual harassment in Egypt (Figure 8).

Figure 8. Harassmap: Tracking sexual harassment in Egypt using Ushahidi

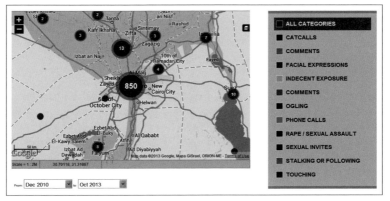

Source: Harassmap.org screenshot

THE LESSONS

Another popular crowdsourcing platform has been designed for translations and surveys. Jana helps companies divide up text-heavy projects and outsource sections to mobile device owners in the developing world for translation in exchange for small remunerations.

The mobile phone has become an important tool for data collection, and it takes on an added dimension when coupled with sensor technology. A project in Ghana, for example, could become a model for future scientific data collection. Recently, taxi drivers in the capital, Accra, were equipped with sensors on their mobile phones, which relayed real-time measurements of carbon levels that were later mapped. As a result, municipalities were able to see when and where pollution was becoming concentrated.

The Facebook and Twitter effect

If Facebook was a country, its numbers
would make it the third-largest on earth.

The Internet and social media are one and the same for many people in the developing world. Facebook has more users in developing countries than in the developed world. Jakarta has become Twitter's international capital, as the city that posts the most tweets, according to the Paris-based research firm Semiocast.

Debates abound about the role of social media in development, ranging from quasi-euphoric optimism over social media's role in spurring democratization and facilitating community development to outright dismissal due to their role in promoting idleness and shallow conversations. As is often the case, the truth lies somewhere in between.

Threats in an increasingly networked world

Although the digital era has certainly created opportunities around the world, concern is growing over whether it could also exacerbate problems in developing countries.

New forms of exclusion

As we saw in previous chapters, daily activities — from accessing social services to gaining a competitive advantage — increasingly require digital capability. People who lack access to the Internet or a mobile device are excluded from these benefits. Women and the disabled, traditionally on the margins of the digital world, will likely be most at risk of exclusion.

Creative destruction, innovation, and intellectual property

The Internet allows for infinite reproduction of some materials at little or no cost. Creative industries, such as music, publishing, and film, are being transformed as a result. However, the socioeconomic ramifications of this transformation have not yet completely emerged. Will opportunities to innovate, hire, and generate revenue in these industries increase or decrease with the growth of digital media?

Intellectual property constitutes a vital part of this new paradigm as the rules surrounding it determine who may use and control the most important assets of networked societies, namely technology and knowledge. Traditional assumptions need to be questioned — for example, that greater protection of intellectual property yields greater development or that the number of patents filed indicates the rate of innovation. These relationships are complex and have become more so in networked economies.

Intellectual property rules generally tend to favour the establishment. James Boyle (2004) points out an inherent hypocrisy in the protection granted to intellectual property holders in developed countries. "The countries that now preach the virtues of expansive minimum levels of intellectual property protection, did not themselves follow that path to industrial development," he observes.

The 2011 Anti-Counterfeiting Trade Agreement, signed by 41 countries, has raised questions among intellectual property scholars about the extent to which it can balance the rights of creators with those of consumers.

Commerce benefiting from flexibilities in intellectual property laws, notably fair use, had an estimated value to the US economy in 2009 of US$4.6 trillion. Google, for example, benefits from flexibilities in intellectual property laws by allowing its users to search for content without being required to systematically seek copyright permissions. The magnitude of this figure shows how important it is to strike a balance between the intellectual property rights of creators and consumers. In practice, such rights are strongly concentrated in rich countries, causing a huge economic divide between the global North and South.

The rise of cyber warfare

Although technology can empower citizens, particularly in authoritarian regimes, the authorities have also been empowered. Many states have become adept at exploiting the benefits of technology. Digital technologies, such as video surveillance, biometric identity scanners, and radio frequency identification tags, have introduced fresh concerns about the surveillance capabilities of governments and corporations. Censorship has also been facilitated by technology and runs rampant in cyberspace.

Dictatorships have exploited the tools people use in the developing world to communicate with each other. Following protests in 2009, the Iranian government cracked down on protesters by capturing data that had been sent from mobile phones to social media sites. During the Tunisian protests of late 2010 and early 2011, which sparked the Arab Spring, the Tunisian government allegedly created fake Facebook, Twitter, and Gmail sites so that unwitting protesters would log on and be identified. In an age where computers can store vast amounts of data, and video surveillance and biometric identity scanners are becoming prevalent, the ability of states and corporations to monitor citizens has given rise to increasing concern.

The Internet "has become the fifth domain of warfare, after land, sea, air and space," notes *The Economist* (2010). This new theatre of operations includes just-in-time election blocking, computer network attacks, patriotic "hacktivists," targeted surveillance, and social malware.

Privacy is dead

Even in democratic countries, government concern about security has put increasing strain on the protection of privacy rights. In India, for example, a biometric identification system requires everyone over 15 to be photographed, fingerprinted, and subjected to an iris scan. This and other personal information is entered into a national database. Privacy is also under threat from corporations such as Facebook that seek to use individuals' data for advertising and other corporate interests. This is especially troubling at a time when computers are able to permanently store records of everything.

Information and Networks program: IDRC's role

In this book, we have identified a number of trends that are deemed important to the future role of ICTs in development. One of these is the explosive growth of mobile phones, which continues to make digital access less challenging and to open up new ways for people to access information and collaborate.

Some groups, however, are still being marginalized. The Gender Research for African Community Empowerment network has expressed concern that women are not participating as much as they could in emerging networked societies. With technology increasingly important in all facets of society, much more needs to be learned about how information networks affect socio-economic inclusion.

Digital openness, privacy, censorship, and intellectual property are all important policy issues that arise from new technology and merit serious research. IDRC has responded to this need with its Information and Networks program. It aims to support critical Southern perspectives and to promote inclusive and beneficial uses of open and digital platforms. The program focuses on three principal areas:

➤ Harnessing the openness of networked technologies

➤ Protecting citizens' rights

➤ Helping marginalized communities benefit from digital technologies.

Digital information can now be accessed, produced, used, reused, and shared around the world at little cost. New ways of organizing and producing information have also emerged, such as free and open-source software and Wikipedia-like crowdsourcing. These collaborative processes have spread throughout the creative economy and the spheres of science, government, and learning. Ushahidi applications are also having a significant impact in many places. In Mexico, for example, Cuidemos el Voto enabled citizens to report incidents of fraud in the electoral process, resulting in 335 official investigations.

IDRC will continue to contribute in important ways in this area, by working to increase openness, enhance information, and move ICT research into the mainstream. Many questions remain to be answered. For example:

➤ Do open educational resources, such as Khan Academy, help improve the quality of learning as well as access to education?

➤ How are entrepreneurs in developing regions making use of open business models to create vibrant, dynamic, knowledge-intensive services and industries?

➤ How can open access to research findings and data enhance the production, uptake, and quality of research results?

➤ With new sources of data being collected from ubiquitous digital sources — mobile phones, GPS devices, ATM machines, and surveillance cameras, among others — how will legislators balance opportunities for increased security and business ventures with the protection of privacy?

Just a few questions for the interesting times ahead.

Glossary of terms and abbreviations

Bottom of the pyramid (BoP/BOP) — Describes the largest and lowest income bracket. Some researchers use the term to refer to people living on less than US$1.25 a day, while others use the cut-off of US$2.50 a day.

Digital divide — The social and economic gap that exists between people who own or have good access to information and communication technology and those with little or no access or familiarity.

DIRSI — Diálogo Regional sobre Sociedad de la Información. Research network in Latin America that focuses on ICT policy, regulation, and governance.

ECLAC — United Nations Economic Commission for Latin America and the Caribbean

ICT — Information and communication technology

ICT4D — Information and communication technologies for development. A sub-specialty for academics and activists who study technology in a development context and believe that conditions in the developing world can be improved by increasing access to technology.

ITU — International Telecommunication Union

LIRNEasia — Learning Initiatives on Reforms for Network Economies Asia. ICT policy and regulation think tank active across the Asia-Pacific region.

NSO — National statistics office

OECD — Organisation for Economic Co-operation and Development

OSILAC — Observatory for the Information Society in Latin America and the Caribbean

PICTURE Africa — Poverty and ICTs in Urban and Rural Eastern Africa. A research project investigating the links between poverty and ICTs.

RIA — Research ICT Africa. A South Africa-based network that conducts research on ICT policy and regulation.

SMS — Short message service or texting

Sources and resources

Publications

Agüero, A. 2008. Telecommunications expenditure in Peruvian households. DIRSI, Lima, Peru, and IDRC, Ottawa, Canada.

Agüero, A.; de Silva, H.; Kang, J. 2011. Bottom of the pyramid expenditure patterns on mobile services in selected emerging Asian countries. *Information Technologies & International Development, 7*(3).

Alterna Perú. 2008. Impacto en el desarrollo económico y social de la telefonía celular en la provincia de Canas. Alterna Perú, Lima, Peru.

Ban Ki-moon. 2012. Poverty eradication: Report of the Secretary-General. United Nations, 1 Feb.

Barrantes, R.; Galperin, H. 2008. Can the poor afford mobile telephony? Evidence from Latin America. *Telecommunications Policy, 32*(8): 521-530.

Bonina, C.M.; Illa, M.R. 2008. Mobile telephony and digital poverty in Latin America: Can the expansion of cellular telephones reduce poverty? DIRSI, Lima, Peru, and IDRC, Ottawa, Canada.

Boyle, J. 2004. A manifesto on WIPO and the future of intellectual property. *Duke Law & Technology Review, 3*: 1–13.

Calandro, E.; Stork, C.; Gillwald, A. 2012. Internet going mobile: Internet access and usage in 11 African countries. Research ICT Africa, Cape Town, South Africa.

Chakraborty, D. 2004. The case of mobile phones in Sitakund. *i4d, 2*(5): 14-17.

Cooke, A. 2012. Deep read: tweeting out of poverty. *Mail & Guardian*, 22 Oct.

De Angoitia, R.; Ramirez, F. 2008. Cost-reduction strategies employed by mobile telephony users in low-income sectors in Mexico. DIRSI, Lima, Peru, and IDRC, Ottawa, Canada.

De Angoitia, R.; Ramirez, F. 2009. Strategic use of mobile telephony at the bottom of the pyramid: the case of Mexico. *Information Technologies & International Development, 5*(3): 35–53.

Deen-Swarray, M.; Gillwald, A.; Morrell, A. 2013. Lifting the veil on ICT gender indicators in Africa. Research ICT Africa, Cape Town, South Africa.

De Los Ríos, C. 2010. Impacto del uso de internet en el bienestar de los hogares peruanos: evidencia de un panel de hogares, 2007–2009. DIRSI, Lima, Peru, and IDRC, Ottawa, Canada.

De Silva, H.; Zainudeen, A. 2008. Teleuse at the bottom of the pyramid: beyond universal access. *Telektronikk, 2*: 25–38.

Diga, K. 2013. The nexus between poverty and ICTs. In Elder, L.; Emdon, H.; Fuchs, R.; Petrazzini, B. (editors). *Connecting ICTs to development: the IDRC experience*. Anthem Press, London, UK, and IDRC, Ottawa, Canada.

Duncombe, R. 2006. Using the livelihoods framework to analyze ICT applications for poverty reduction through microenterprise. *Information Technologies and International Development*, 3(3): 81–100.

Economist, The. 2010. Cyberwar: the threat from the Internet. 1 July.

Flores-Roux, E.; Renteria, C. 2013. The welfare impact of broadband in Mexico. DIRSI, Lima, Peru, and IDRC, Ottawa, Canada.

Galpaya, H. 2012. Apps for the agriculture value chain. Presented at the 5th international ICTD conference, 12–15 March 2012, Atlanta, USA.

Galperin, H. 2012. Prices and quality of broadband in Latin America: benchmarking and trends. Universidad de San Andrés Centro de Tecnologia y Sociedad. Working paper 12.

Galperin, H.; Mariscal, J. (editors). 2007. *Digital poverty: Latin American and Caribbean perspectives.* Practical Action Publishing, Rugby, UK, and IDRC, Ottawa, Canada.

Galperin, H.; Mariscal, J. 2007. Mobile opportunities: poverty and mobile telephony in Latin America and the Caribbean. DIRSI, Lima, Peru, and IDRC, Ottawa, Canada.

Gillwald, A.; Milek, A.; Stork, C. 2010. Towards evidence-based ICT policy and regulation: gender assessment of ICT access and usage in Africa. Research ICT Africa, Cape Town, South Africa.

Gillwald, A.; Stork, C. 2008. Towards evidence-based ICT policy and regulation: ICT access and usage in Africa. Research ICT Africa, Cape Town, South Africa.

Grimshaw, D.J.; Kala, S. (editors). 2011. *Strengthening rural livelihoods: the impact of information and communication technologies in Asia.* Practical Action Publishing, Rugby, UK, and IDRC, Ottawa, Canada.

Herath, M.B. 2008. High AMPU from low ARPU. In Samarajiva, R.; Zainudeen, A. (editors). *ICT infrastructure in emerging Asia: policy and regulatory roadblocks.* IDRC, Ottawa, Canada, and Sage Publications, New Delhi, India.

International Telecommunication Union. 2012. ICT-Eye: key ICT data and statistics. ITU website, Geneva, Switzerland.

International Telecommunication Union. 2012. *Measuring the information society.* ITU, Geneva, Switzerland.

Jensen, R. 2007. The digital provide: information (technology), market performance, and welfare in the South Indian fisheries sector. *The Quarterly Journal of Economics, 122*(3): 879–924.

Jordán, V.; Galperin, H.; Peres, W. (editors). 2011. *Fast-tracking the digital revolution: broadband for Latin America and the Caribbean.* ECLAC, Santiago, Chile.

Jordán, V.; Galperin, H.; Peres, W. (editors). 2013. *Broadband in Latin America: beyond connectivity.* ECLAC, Santiago, Chile.

Kang, J.; Maity, M. 2012. Texting among the bottom of the pyramid: facilitators and barriers to SMS use among the low-income mobile users in Asia. LIRNE*asia*, Colombo, Sri Lanka.

Katz, R.; Callorda, F. 2013. The economic impact of broadband deployment in Ecuador. DIRSI, Lima, Peru, and IDRC, Ottawa, Canada.

Knight-John, Malathy. 2008. Making a business out of a village phone. In Samarajiva, R.; Zainudeen, A. (editors). *ICT infrastructure in emerging Asia: policy and regulatory roadblocks*. IDRC, Ottawa, Canada, and Sage Publications, New Delhi, India.

Lokanathan, S., de Silva, H. and Fernando, I. 2011. Price transparency in agricultural produce markets: Sri Lanka. In D. J. Grimshaw and S. Kala (Eds), *Strengthening rural livelihoods: the impact of information and communication technologies in Asia*. Practical Action Publishing, Rugby, UK, and IDRC, Ottawa, Canada.

Mariscal, J. 2009. Mobiles for development: M-banking. Presented at the XXVIII International Congress of the Latin American Studies Association, 11–14 June 2009, Rio de Janeiro, Brazil.

Mariscal, J.; Martinez, M. 2013. The informational lives of the poor: a pilot study in three Mexican communities. DIRSI, Lima, Peru, and IDRC, Ottawa, Canada.

May, J; Adera, E. 2011. The ICT/poverty nexus. *UN Chronicle Online*, 2011, XLVIII(3).

May, J.; Dutton, V.; Munyakazi, L. n.d. Information and communication technologies as an escape from poverty traps: evidence from East Africa. PICTURE Africa, IDRC, Ottawa, Canada.

Qiang, C.Z.W. 2009. Mobile telephony: a transformational tool for growth and development. *Private Sector & Development*, Issue 4 (November).

Samarajiva, R., 2010. Leveraging the budget telecom network business model to bring broadband to the people. *Information Technologies & International Development, 6 (special ed)*.

Samarajiva, R., 2011. Mobile at the bottom of the pyramid: informing policy from the demand side. *Information Technologies & International Development, 7*(3).

Samarajiva, R. 2011. Teleuse@BOP4: preliminary findings. LIRNE*asia*, Colombo, Sri Lanka.

Samarajiva, R. 2012. What do we know about the teleuse of those "not like us"? Presented at the 5th international ICTD conference, 12–15 March 2012, Atlanta, USA.

Samarajiva, R.; Gamage, S. 2007. Bridging the divide: building Asia-Pacific capacity for effective reforms. *The Information Society, 23*(2): 109–117.

Samarajiva, R.; Zainudeen, A. (editors). 2008. *ICT infrastructure in emerging Asia: policy and regulatory roadblocks.* IDRC, Ottawa, Canada, and Sage Publications, New Delhi, India.

Shaffer, R. 2007. Unplanned obsolescence. *Fast Company,* September 2007.

Smith, M.L.; Spence, R.; Rashid, A.T. 2011. Mobile phones and expanding human capabilities. *Information Technologies & International Development, 7*(3): 77–88.

Smith, P. 2011. Stories from across Namibia. Research ICT Africa, Cape Town, South Africa. Unpublished.

Sridhar, K.S.; Sridhar, V. 2007. Telecommunications infrastructure and economic growth: evidence from developing countries. National Institute of Public Finance and Policy, New Delhi, India. Working paper 04/14.

Stork, C. 2012. Mobile money — what's next? Presented at the 5th international ICTD conference, 12–15 March 2012, Atlanta, USA. Teleuse@BOP3. 2009. LIRNE*asia* website, Colombo, Sri Lanka.

Torero, M.; Von Braun, J. 2006. Impacts of ICT on low-income rural households. In Torero, M.; Von Braun, J. (editors). *Information and communication technologies for development and poverty reduction: the potential of telecommunications.* Johns Hopkins University Press, Baltimore, USA.

Vergara, S.; Rovira, S.; Balboni, M. 2011. *ICT in Latin America: a microdata analysis.* ECLAC, Santiago, Chile, and IDRC, Ottawa, Canada.

Waverman, L.; Meschi, M.; Fuss, M.A. 2005. The impact of telecoms on economic growth in developing countries. In *Africa: the impact of mobile phones.* Vodafone Group, Newbury, UK.

World Bank. 2010. At the tipping point: The implications of Kenya's ICT revolution. *Kenya economic update* (edition 3). World Bank, Washington, DC, USA.

World Bank. 2013. Migration and Development Brief. World Bank, Washington, DC, USA.

Zainudeen, A. 2008. What do users at the bottom of the pyramid want? In Samarajiva, R.; Zainudeen, A. (editors). 2008. *ICT infrastructure in emerging Asia: policy and regulatory roadblocks.* IDRC, Ottawa, Canada, and Sage Publications, New Delhi, India.

Zainudeen, A.; Iqbal, T. 2008. Strategies on a shoestring. In Samarajiva, R.; Zainudeen, A. (editors). *ICT infrastructure in emerging Asia: policy and regulatory roadblocks.* IDRC, Ottawa, Canada, and Sage Publications, New Delhi, India.

Zainudeen, A.; Iqbal, T.; Samarajiva, R. 2010. Who's got the phone? Gender and the use of the telephone at the bottom of the pyramid. *New Media & Society, 12*(4): 549–566.

Research networks

This book draws on unique household surveys and in-depth studies undertaken with IDRC support in Africa, Asia, and Latin America. Interested readers can find a rich trove of research findings and analysis on the websites of the regional networks that conducted the surveys.

Diálogo Regional sobre Sociedad de la Información (DIRSI): dirsi.net/en

Learning Initiatives on Reforms for Network Economies Asia (LIRNE*asia*): lirneasia.net

Research ICT Africa (RIA): researchictafrica.net

The Publisher

Canada's International Development Research Centre (IDRC) funds practical research in developing countries to increase prosperity and security, and to foster democracy and the rule of law, in support of Canada's international development efforts. We promote growth and development and encourage sharing knowledge with policymakers, other researchers, and communities around the world. The result is innovative, lasting solutions that aim to bring change to those who need it most.

IDRC Books publishes research results and scholarly studies on global and regional issues related to sustainable and equitable development. As a specialist in development literature, IDRC Books contributes to the body of knowledge on these issues to further the cause of global understanding and equity. The full catalogue is available at **www.idrc.ca/books**.